CONVERSATIONS
WITH AN
UNREPENTANT
LIBERAL

CONVERSATIONS
WITH AN
UNREPENTANT
LIBERAL

BY

JULIUS SEELYE BIXLER

KENNIKAT PRESS
Port Washington, N. Y./London

CONVERSATIONS WITH AN UNREPENTANT LIBERAL

Copyright © 1946 by Yale University Press
Reprinted 1973 by Kennikat Press in an
unabridged and unaltered edition with permission
Library of Congress Catalog Card No.: 72-85298
ISBN 0-8046-1713-9

Manufactured by Taylor Publishing Company   Dallas, Texas

To

ELIZABETH

THE DWIGHT HARRINGTON TERRY FOUNDATION

Lectures on Religion in the Light of Science and Philosophy

This volume is based upon the twenty-second series of lectures delivered at Yale University on the Foundation established by the late Dwight H. Terry of Bridgeport, Connecticut, through his gift of $100,000 as an endowment fund for the delivery and subsequent publication of "Lectures on Religion in the Light of Science and Philosophy."

The deed of gift declares that "the object of this Foundation is not the promotion of scientific investigation and discovery, but rather the assimilation and interpretation of that which has been or shall be hereafter discovered, and its application to human welfare, especially by the building of the truths of science and philosophy into the structure of a broadened and purified religion. The founder believes that such a religion will greatly stimulate intelligent effort for the improvement of human conditions and the advancement of the race in strength and excellence of character. To this end it is desired that lectures or a series of lectures be given by men eminent in their respective departments, on ethics, the history of civilization and religion, biblical research, all sciences and branches of knowledge which have an important bearing on the subject, all the great laws of nature, especially of evolution . . . also such interpretations of literature and sociology as are in accord with the spirit of this Foundation, to the end that the Christian spirit may be nurtured in the fullest light of the world's knowledge and that mankind may be helped to attain its highest possible welfare and happiness upon this earth . . .

"The lectures shall be subject to no philosophical or religious test and no one who is an earnest seeker after truth shall be excluded because his views seem radical or destructive of existing

*beliefs. The founder realizes that the liberalism of one generation
is often conservatism in the next, and that many an apostle of true
liberty has suffered martyrdom at the hands of the orthodox. He
therefore lays special emphasis on complete freedom of utterance,
and would welcome expressions of conviction from sincere thinkers of differing standpoints even when these may run counter to
the generally accepted views of the day. The founder stipulates
only that the managers of the fund shall be satisfied that the
lecturers are well qualified for their work and are in harmony
with the cardinal principles of the Foundation, which are loyalty
to the truth, lead where it will, and devotion to human welfare."*

PREFACE

THE founder realizes that the liberalism of one generation is often conservatism in the next," says the deed of gift for this lectureship. "He therefore lays special emphasis on complete freedom of utterance, and would welcome expressions of conviction . . . even when these may run counter to the generally accepted views of the day." Was the liberal ideal ever more felicitously expressed? And is it conceivable that the interpretation of freedom as based on this kind of generous tolerance toward dissenting opinions should ever fail to find favor among thoughtful people?

Hard as it is to realize, liberalism is seriously challenged today and the liberal tradition is itself at bay. In the bitterness of the postwar mood many of our contemporaries are unwilling to accept the liberal's view of freedom as meaning anything else than a lack of conviction, while his readiness to look for truth in what is new and untried appears merely as the first step toward a color-blind relativism.

The liberal would be unfaithful to his own deepest insights if he should refuse to listen to his critics. Particularly in this day of the ascendancy of physical force he should be very certain of his ground before claiming too much for the methods of reasonable persuasion. It is entirely possible that his eagerness for discussion may mask his own fear of action and his inability to make up his mind. When there is so much to do and so little time in which to do it the desire to hear all sides of every question may be merely the sign of a dilatory disposition.

Yet to say this is to state the worst of the case against the liberal and this, it would seem, is a criticism of him as a person rather than of his philosophy. If the ideas of liberalism have been used by some as an excuse for avoiding action the obligation on others is the greater to make sure of their own motives in adopting it. No philosophy is proof against abuse from its adherents. The fact that evil is often done in the name of good does not make the good evil. Freedom is a conception the full meaning of which we have not yet grasped. As democracy struggles with this problem it needs the help of liberalism in the sense in which a political and economic theory needs the backing of a more inclusive philosophical attitude.

We need the liberal, then, because of his special insights into the nature of freedom, and we need him also because of his devotion to peace. In other periods of history it may have been true that the times called for those who put the joys of partisan struggle high on their list of values. But today not only does the whole world yearn for peace—it knows that the alternative is annihilation. The liberal has a significant message for our age since at heart he is not a party member or a defender of a special creed but one who feels the unity of the human cause and the commonness of the human aim. Sometimes his interest in what is universal has seemed to remove him from our problems in their stark particularity. But as we return today to the larger view and feel the growing pains of one world in the making the relevance of the liberal's contribution becomes more clear.

Something of the same sort is true, I think, of the liberal's reliance on reason. In one sense the appeal to reason is so vague as to be meaningless. But our protest against its vagueness has gone so far that we are beginning to lose our sense for what reason can do. This seems especially to be the case in our thought about religion. The pendulum has swung a long way toward irrationalism in contemporary theology and the balance of the liberal is sorely needed. "We indeed grant that the use of reason in religion is accompanied with danger," said Channing in his Baltimore sermon of 1819. "But we ask any honest man," he went on, "to look back on the history of the church and say, whether the renunciation of it be not still more dangerous."

What we should remember about liberalism is that it offers not so much a final solution as a starting point and an indication of a general direction to be followed. It fixes our attention on universal and unquestionable values and, because it cannot claim to furnish specific solutions for all our ills, it should always be supplemented by a study of the concrete particular. With this in mind I have put these lectures in the form of a conversation where the liberal appeals to general ideas and his friend and critic tries to make him face hard and specific facts. For characters I have ventured to bring Simmias and Cebes out of the Greek classroom where some of us first became acquainted with them and to confront them with a few of our problems of the present. We have known them as witnesses, while visitors in a prison, of one of the great dramatic events of history. The question now is how far they can become participants in the drama of today. Professor Howard M. Jones has well said that the liberal should be made to face the dilemmas of the local situation and the issues of home-town politics. In the conversations that follow Simmias and Cebes may still find them-selves unable to come successfully to grips with what is familiar and immediate but at least their environment is such as to bring it to their notice.

It is hard to know where to stop in acknowledging indebt-edness for ideas used even in a brief course of lectures such as this. I have drawn on many sources but special mention should be made of the following books that have recently appeared: *The Children of Light and the Children of Dark-ness* by Reinhold Niebuhr, *Diagnosis of our Time* by Karl Mannheim, *God and Evil* by C. E. M. Joad, *The Uses of Reason* by Arthur E. Murphy, *Philosophical Understanding and Religious Truth* by Erich Frank, *The Decline of Liber-alism as an Ideology* by John H. Hallowell, *Politics and Morals* by Benedetto Croce, and *The Changing Reputation of Human Nature* by James Luther Adams. I am also in-debted to the editors of the following publications for allow-ing quotations from articles of mine that have appeared in the last few years: *The Philosophical Review, The Review of Religion,* the *Crozer Quarterly,* and *The Harvard Teachers' Record* (now *The Harvard Educational Review*). Professor Edgar S. Brightman and Dr. Jannette E. Newhall have been kind enough to read the manuscript and their suggestions have been gratefully received.

J.S.B.

Colby College
Waterville, Maine
January 1, 1946

CONTENTS

THE LIBERAL AT BAY

A LONG time ago, in ancient Athens, Simmias and Cebes spent many hours discussing the great problems of life and death, including the question of reincarnation. Their guess that it is possible is verified in the twentieth century A.D. In the year 1945 they are discovered, however, not in the Elysian Fields, where they had hoped to be, but eating breakfast at a lunch counter in the North Station in Boston. Their friendship in the present incarnation has again extended over many years but they realize that whereas in their personal feeling for each other they are no less close than formerly, the more rapid tempo of modern life has somewhat sharpened their differences of opinion on the moot topics of religion and education. Experience in this incarnation has taught them also that they are no longer pawns in the hands of a master but are simply men of average intelligence, with perhaps slightly more than average good will, who are trying to face honestly the problems of the terrifying new world into which they have been plunged.

Simmias was for some years a college teacher of economics, but the recent migration of professors to Washington has engulfed him, and he is now on the government's pay roll. He is delighted with his new position of leadership and is inclined to look down on his former occupation as both prosaic and ineffective. He retains, however, his lifelong admiration for John Dewey as the professor-reformer for whom teaching has never been used as a means of escape and for whom words and ideas are really weapons in the social struggle. The one criticism he makes of Dewey is that his revolt against intrenched reactionary forces both in society and philosophy has not gone far enough. Dewey, he thinks, still reveals a sentimental longing for metaphysics and an unfortunate refusal to come out flatly in favor of positivism or the scientific view that knowledge is won only through the senses. Dewey's attitude toward religion is also, he feels, a trifle ambiguous. At times he seems to wash his hands of it or to rail against it as a nuisance. But at other times he appears to try to fit his thought into the molds that religion has made familiar and has even gone so far as to lecture on foundations established under its auspices. Simmias can only explain this as an unhappy vestige of the "liberalism" that for the most part he has outgrown.

Simmias admits that in his own thinking religion presents an issue that is most baffling. He has no use for metaphysics; he is thoroughly convinced that science alone opens the gate to knowledge; yet he is by temperament a reformer and he admits that some types of religion have brought with them an unparalleled zeal for reform. Like many of his contemporaries he finds a practical solution in the attitude of revolt and especially in the strength of his hatred for that against which he revolts. What he really cannot stand, he tells himself, is the fatuous way in which the liberal clings to his belief in reasonable methods of persuasion when the world is so obviously ruled by violent force. He has come finally to the view that his desire for the realism of science, his eagerness for direct reform, and his sympathy for the kind of religion that gets things done have a common root in his antipathy for the evasions of liberalism, and that he can accept religion so long as he is sure that it is not of the liberal type. After all, he says, a truly rugged religion relies on faith, which is not the same as the liberal's reliance on reason, and there is no inconsistency in combining faith with scientific positivism so long as one recognizes frankly that faith and reason are completely different. Thus like many of his contemporaries Simmias has begun to pride himself on his use of a negative attitude of revolt as a guide to a positive core of belief.

Cebes teaches religion in a small college in the state of Maine. He still calls himself a liberal because he cannot find any other label that comes so near to describing his deepest convictions. But when questioned he admits that his confidence in the methods of liberalism has been dealt a staggering blow. Sometimes he blames liberalism for apathy or lack of vision or sheer cowardice. At other times he is sure that these faults are in himself rather than in the liberal ideal. Occasionally he plucks up courage to hope that liberalism can become sufficiently dynamic to enable even his frail nature to confront a world ravaged by war. But he is frank to confess that his own capacity for making moral decisions will need considerable strengthening. Cebes is of a reflective temperament, with somewhat classical and formal tastes. This does not prevent him from having very strong feelings, but he has trouble when he tries to translate them into action and to turn them to practical account. More often than he likes to admit he is a tortured soul who agonizes over the problems of society without doing anything to solve them except to contribute from time to time a rather wordy article or lecture.

The two have just come in on the night train from Maine,

where Simmias had exhorted a somewhat unruly group at the college where Cebes teaches. They are traveling together as far as New Haven with stopovers to visit libraries at the university cities of Cambridge and Providence. At the lunch counter they converse in the midst of escaping steam, clanging bells, and all the frantic rush of station traffic. After watching the hectic activities of the crowd for a few minutes Simmias takes up a subject that has always interested him.

———————

Whatever else we may think of it, Simmias remarked, the passing of the age of gasoline with the return to the age of steam has restored some of the color and drama of travel. Surely there is more excitement in meeting your friend at a bustling railroad station than in watching him glide quietly up to your front doorstep. I should think, also, that you would prefer to have your college year begin with the arrival of a noisy mob of students giving vent to their enthusiasm as they flock off the train, instead of having them come unobtrusively in automobile loads of two's and three's.

Furthermore, there is a kind of social symbolism about train travel, he observed. Along with other passengers you dash madly through the gates, ask the brakeman which car to take, scramble aboard, stow your luggage, and settle yourself in a seat by the window on the shady side before the other fellow can get there. It is a perfect example of the ruthless and breathless competition which takes up so much of our effort. Then when the train starts you realize how completely your interests are bound up with those of your fellow passengers. Your hopes and fears are the same; what happens to one happens to all. It would be hard to find a better example of the limits of individualism. I should therefore welcome this return to the dramatic age of steam were it not for the prominence it gives to the drama's tragic side. Take those scenes over there on the platform, for example. The newly drafted men in that column of two's are putting up a brave front but I hate to think of what is going on within. The mother at the gate has a courageous smile, but the tears will come soon enough. A railroad station brings us face to face with the fact that life is but a succession of partings from what has come to be loved.

You talk as if you'd just been reading Buddhist literature, said Cebes. Of course life has its partings, but it has its meetings also.

Yes, but you meet after you have parted, replied Simmias, and you meet only to part again. War simply emphasizes how large a role separation plays in experience as we know it. The few brief days of an army leave remind us that the moments of life we enjoy are but transient gleams against a background of unrelieved darkness. Even now the hospital trains and ambulances are out in the yard and although they are invisible to us their presence colors the entire scene.

In fact, he continued, all the more optimistic philosophies and all the more genteel traditions today are at bay. Struggle and agony are too obviously parts of the daily round, and the attempt to gloss over the cruder phases of existence is no longer possible. This impatience with the refinements by which society has tried to hide life in the raw shows itself in many ways. For example, the younger generation, whose presence was so conspicuous on the train last night, was not brought up, as we were, to hide its feelings of the moment or even to restrain its less polite impulses. It makes love in public. It gives vent to its feelings in short and pithy words which still sound strange to our middle-aged ears. It will not be preached to nor will it allow itself to talk about virtue. In spite of this I should be the first to admit that it lives dangerously and on the whole far more honestly and creditably than we did when we were young. But today's circumstances have forced it to live for the feeling of the moment instead of for the idea that reaches beyond the momentary experience. It lives with more realistic courage than you or I have ever shown, but perhaps with less awareness of some of life's amenities. The result is that it has little use for the labels, the general ideas, the conventional rules, the wordy refinements on which we were brought up. It lives to feel and to act and, especially in the present emergency, it does not dare to think. In other words it represents a social situation where liberalism is dead.

What do you mean by liberalism? asked Cebes somewhat absently, without looking up from his morning newspaper.

As you well know, replied Simmias, with the suggestion of a twinkle in his eyes, the difference between a fool and a wise man is that the former requires a definition at the start, while the latter is willing to wait until the end of a discussion. But just to humor you I'll point to one or two qualities that the liberal always has. In the first place, the liberal, like yourself, is easy to get along with. He is a tolerant, generous person who prides himself on his broadmindedness. He is a man of ideas with confidence in reason as a force in human affairs. Yet although he may at first appear to have all the virtues he turns out to be the victim of some very serious vices. His tolerance is really nothing but a cloak for his underlying skepticism. His hospitality to ideas is a sign of lack of discrimination and evidence of a color-blind type of neutrality. His supposed broadmindedness means lack of intellectual backbone and an unwillingness to take responsibility for making moral decisions. You will recall that Dostoievsky pictures the devil as a liberal; that is, as a charming gentleman whose one fault is that he is wholly unable to make up his mind. Santayana, also, was at his best when he spoke of liberalism as opening to men "that sweet, scholarly, tenderly moral, critically superior attitude of mind which Matthew Arnold called culture." I should express it by saying that the liberal is an unseeing optimist in a world of tragedy, a weak-willed rationalist in a society governed by force, a self-styled humble follower of the truth who is full of intellectual pride, and an escapist who uses his much-vaunted detachment as an excuse for failure to act.

You see that I become rather bitter over the liberals, he continued, because they claim to be so intellectual, and to know so much, when actually they understand so little. They don't seem to realize that the old liberal interest in the free play of economic forces led to the control of the means of production by a privileged group of property owners and brought, therefore, not freedom but bondage. As one writer has said, the freedoms of the past have brought forth the slaveries of the present. Liberals appear not to understand that Locke's phrases about the rights of man are perverted in present-day parlance and used to apply to the special rights of the businessman. They are unaware of the demonic forces at work in society and they overlook the sin in their own hearts. They are as blind to the fall of Adam Smith as to that of Adam. Liberalism really reflects the thinking of an age when men believed they saw the laws of reason at work in both nature and society and supposed that only a little more education was needed to bring perfection to the most reasonable of possible worlds. Even today our liberals still talk blandly of ignorance and maladjustment in the naïve belief that a slight increase in knowledge will turn the trick. On the one hand they profess to believe that ideas can control human nature—as if the passions of a competitive society would show a gentle docility when brought before the bar of reason. On the other they profess to believe that their own ideas can reach up to touch and even encompass the Power that controls the universe—as if God in his majestic might and unutterable sublimity could be brought within the confines of our miserably limited knowledge. In a paroxysm of agony greater than any other age has ever known, our generation cries out for help from on high. In answer what does the liberal do but counsel it to contemplate its own ideas of goodness and beauty!

Of course there's another side to the argument that you haven't mentioned, said Cebes, somewhat ineffectually.

Any student can see how liberalism arose, Simmias continued, but to observe the circumstances of its birth is to make one aware of the inevitability of its death. Liberalism comes from an age different from ours and provides answers to questions other than those asked by our generation. It stems from a time when men were greatly concerned over natural rights and over the conflict between their creative freedom as persons and an impersonal authority in both religion and politics. Earlier, during the Middle Ages, this conflict did not arise. The supreme authority was then vested in a personal God and all men knew that their own highest good would come from submitting themselves to his sovereign will. But in the eighteenth century, just when men began to be interested in themselves as personalities and in their rights as free beings, along came the philosophy of Deism with its account of a God who was impersonal. At the same time the rise of national secular states brought an impersonal authority into politics. As a result, thoughtful people began to ask: To what kind of authority should a free personality submit? This is the question liberalism set itself to answer. It said: The only impersonal authority a free man can recognize is that of eternal reason. Man is free, nature is reasonable, and the chief end of man is to live according to reasonable nature in a society whose laws and institutions represent the unfolding of a rational purpose. In this way the old question of reason versus desire, that we used to debate in ancient Athens, was sharpened and made relevant to the institutions and the environment in which the debaters actually lived.

But now the institutions have changed and the environment is different and our view of the free man and his powers has been profoundly modified. In these days of international cartels and gigantic monopolies free enterprise doesn't mean what it did. The once proud creative spirit so clearly a captain of its purposeful soul has become a sort of passive electron played upon by the various influences of an economic field of force, or an atom pushed hither and yon by the compulsions of the social molecule. In their turn the overarching laws of eternal reason have melted away before the hot breath of our modern scientific positivism. Nature is ruled by mechanical impulses, society is governed by lusts for gain and power so imperious as to be irresistible, and man himself has become an automaton.

Even in its heyday, Simmias went on, liberalism really of-fered a means of criticism rather than a positive approach to life and its problems. Santayana's father was a true liberal when he said, "I don't know what I want; I only know what I don't want." The liberal doesn't like slavery or dogma or war. But who does? T. S. Eliot was right when he remarked that the genius of liberalism was in its "nay-saying" quality. And Laski surely put his finger on its sore spot when he observed that all men know that peace is better than war but that to repeat this now is to offer an incantation instead of a remedy. As he says, liberalism in the face of disaster has merely kept insisting on the value of its procedures which no one doubts but which everyone finds irrelevant. I think it is this fundamental irrelevance of liberalism, Simmias continued, that makes our youth so impatient with it today. Youth is not always articulate about its basic intuitions but some of the intuitions themselves are sure. Among them is its sense for what fits the practical and immediate situation. This is where liberalism falls down. It survives today in a few elderly or middle-aged minds but even there it exists only as a memory, with all passion spent. The most eagerly loyal liberal ought to see that he can't go on believing merely in his own lack of beliefs. It must have been a pleasant dream while it lasted, he added. Whether it is that such a mood makes men easygoing, or whether easygoing men drift naturally into such a mood I wouldn't know, but I do know that its day is past. The moderns have a word that shows it for the vicious farce it is, and the word is "appeasement."

Simmias drew a long breath, wondering whether his feeling had carried him too far, but Cebes, who by this time had laid down his newspaper and was watching the hurrying crowd, did not seem particularly ruffled. You criticize liberalism for being negative, he observed, but I think you are rather negative yourself just at the moment. It is much easier to point out its faults than to show what should be done about them. To me there is something so basic about the view of man as a free being making his decisions in accordance with reason that I find it hard to believe that a philosophy which has this for its central tenet can ever be outgrown. Of course intellectual styles do change. A few years ago we heard only of the struggle of the classes, the economic determination of history, and the coming dictatorship of the proletariat. Today the talk runs to id, libido, and superego. Yet both Marxians and Freudians were exploiting a few special and particularized insights. They may have helped to throw light on certain obscure corners of human life but their ideas never should have been expected to supplant a basic confidence in reason. Did not these people try argument, just as you have been trying it with me? Did they not appeal in the end to the decisions of a reasonable self? Actually, liberalism isn't outworn. It simply needs to be sharpened up a bit and applied in a more specific way to the particular problems of our age. It is significant, I think, that we find today a new concern for democracy which in itself implies a fresh awareness of the permanent qualities in the liberal view. Democracy, as we understand it at present, means liberalism applied to the political field. What we now need to learn is how to make it work in the field of economics. Beyond this immediate and practical issue is the problem of how to work out a theology and a theory of education that will fit our basic rational and democratic loyalties. Wherever we turn, in other words, we need to learn how to apply liberalism instead of giving it up.

What you have said about our discussions of reason as opposed to feeling strikes a responsive chord in me, he continued. I accept the distinction, just as I did in ancient Athens, as one of the most important we can make. To me the essence of liberalism is the view that the reasonable standards, qualities, and relations with which the mind deals in its capacity as judge can be abstracted from the imperious driving desires that make up so much of the stream of experience, and that the judgments made by temporarily abstracting ideas in this way can be used to control conduct and improve it. Ideas do exist apart in a special sense, as Socrates himself used to teach. But I sometimes think that the liberal who sees the glory of the world of ideas and pins his hopes to it is the one who also sees how heavy is the responsibility placed on the man who would be guided by ideas. They are truly apart from much that we feel and do, and we have to reach after them and struggle with them and compel them by main force to come down and live with us. It is characteristic of them that they expect us to use force and will not exert it themselves. They insist on recognizing our freedom and they are quite content to leave us severely alone. This leads me to ask whether we should not blame our ideas or our philosophy or our liberalism less and ourselves and our weak wills more. Although we have seen the better, we have, in our feeble way, pursued the worse, and the problem now is that of disciplining our wills rather than changing our ideas. I would hold that the chief need is to condition our interests and desires rather than to modify our notions of the good and the bad.

To say, then, with you, that liberalism is dead, he concluded, is to say that we do indeed live at the most tragic era of the world's history. But you make me think of Nietzsche's statement about the death of God. God was killed, Nietzsche said, by the essential honesty of men. In that case of course he wasn't dead at all but merely showing himself in a new form. I wonder whether in your turn you may be pointing not to the death of liberalism but to a new line of growth. Until you demonstrate the contrary I shall continue to think of you as a liberal in spite of yourself.

How characteristic of you liberals is that compromise! said Simmias. Oh well, you would say, we're both seeking the same ends, what do the means matter? After all, said the liberal Unitarian to his Anglican friend, we're both doing the Lord's will. Yes, said the Anglican, you in your way, and I in his! Well, from my point of view, the Anglican was both more shrewd and more candid. Your liberal tolerance is really insufferable. For my part, I will not be called an unwitting liberal, or a liberal in spite of myself, when I see so clearly the failure of liberalism today. You give your own case away when you talk, as you did just now, about belief in freedom as an excuse for following inclination rather than ideas. How distressed Socrates would have been to hear such a remark! As you know well enough, Socrates was himself a perfect example of the man who was free just because reasonable ideas controlled him completely. If you aren't careful you'll push me to the point of defending a kind of rationalism I abhor. Incidentally, when you say that reason has no force of its own you point to the essential weakness in the liberal's religion. Of course the object of a man's worship must have force. Of course his own faltering will needs more power from on high. No religion worthy of the name ever preached anything else. But what most disturbs me in your conversation is your obvious misunderstanding of the role of philosophy when at the same time you so constantly parade your special interest in it. I'm beginning to believe that you can't recognize a working philosophy when you see one. It is your opponents, the fascists and the communists, who really have a philosophy of life, not you. They would never admit that men had to woo ideas and plead with them and reach after them. For such people ideas are irresistible forces. Naturally I never could be a fascist, but sometimes I seriously think I'd rather be a communist and say at one moment that ideas are nothing but the echoes of the clash of competing systems if at another I could find, as they seem to, an effective working philosophy where the idea of what is right enters so forcefully into life and dominates it so completely.

The trouble with you liberals boils down to the fact that you aren't really playing the game or fighting the battle. You are content to sit and talk by the fireside while civilization itself sickens and dies. In some ways you remind me of the radio announcer who tries to make the tones of his voice convey the impression that the battle is coming out all right so we needn't worry. Well, it may come out all right for him since he is thousands of miles away, but it is different for those on the scene. Don't you understand that in a society that has lost its health and wholeness your fine-sounding phrases simply make its contradictions more sharp? Just at a time in history when architecture is beginning to show an originality and sensitiveness like that of ours in ancient Greece, whole cities are pulverized; just when science seems about to give men control of nature and to make them truly free, millions are thrown into the worst forms of slavery; just when society begins to be aware of some of its worst ills and to take measures to cure them, civilization does its best to destroy itself. A generation of young people before whom might have stretched the fairest prospect ever to confront the inhabitants of this planet has been sent out to kill its own members and has been taught the lesson that force is finally the arbiter. How can you go on repeating the old formulas in days like these?

So depressed had Simmias become by this time that he moved away from the lunch counter and started, rather absent-mindedly, to put on his overcoat.

I'm not sure that you are aware of what the liberal is doing, remarked Cebes, as he paid for both breakfasts and picked up the bags. The fact is that he believes in making a new start just as much as you do but he doesn't want it to be a false start and he doesn't want to get off on the wrong foot. His trouble, I admit, is that sometimes he hesitates so long that he fails to start at all. But you can't in fairness accuse him of complete unwillingness to act. The social progress and the advance toward freedom of recent years, at which you have yourself hinted, has been made, by and large, under liberal auspices. Of course I don't want to make a fetish of the word "liberalism" or to have it become too much of a partisan slogan. I'm inclined to think that it is unfair to push the liberal into too narrow a corner, as if he were a member of some special sect, and insist on his emerging with a detailed practical program or not at all. There is something to be said for the basic principles on which any program must be built and the liberal is the one who is afraid that in the strife of competing interests these may be forgotten. That is what most distresses me about the revolt against liberalism today. We should not cast it aside until we have explored more thoroughly what it means. Then we should try to bring out its implications for these terribly pressing problems of our time.

For example, you have spoken of the liberal's tolerance as a form of appeasement. The word is a disagreeable one because it suggests compromise with the forces of evil. But our disgust with appeasement should not make us blind to the virtues of tolerance or to its uses even today. The resort to force is the next to the worst of all possible evils and can be excused only when the alternative is dishonor and slavery. And we should remember that tolerance itself does not mean merely a pleasant and pliant openness to every wind of doctrine. There is a kind of tolerance that springs from the presence, not the absence, of convictions. The characteristic intellectual method of our time is that of science, and science ought to show us clearly that a liberal tolerance can become a hardheaded vigorous instrument in the pursuit of truth and the alleviation of human ill. The scientist calls it "experimentalism" and he means a willingness to let each fact stand on its own feet and show what it is worth. In the same way democracy means allowing each man to speak for himself until he speaks against the common good. Now of course in both cases tolerance is kept from being mere wishy-washy acceptance of what is given by the driving purposes that are at work. For science the end is truth; for democracy, justice. But I think that the interest the public shows in both science and democracy rests not merely on a desire for immediately useful facts or a working political scheme. It stands also for a half-articulate conviction that both science and democracy are in line with a profoundly philosophical view which, if rightly apprehended, can bring the salvation all of us are seeking. I mean simply that each applies in its particular field the ideals of reason; and reason, however it may be abused for special purposes, is in its essence an expression of the human passion for universality.

It still seems to me that you're only using long words to hide your own lack of ideas, said Simmias.

No, said Cebes, back of these words I'm sure there is an idea, and you must help me to bring it out. You have doubted whether a view of life which makes so much as does liberalism of the judicial and rational can be either warmhearted or aggressive enough to meet today's demand for action. For my part, I think it can. I believe the crying need today is for a universal view that will lift us out of all partisanships, all dangerous provincialisms and sectarianisms, and that will bind us together in the commonness of our purpose as human beings. Rightly taken, liberalism should do just this. Liberalism pictures men as sharing in a common reason. It is true that they share feelings as well, but it is the differences in human feelings that, when kept under control, give life so much of its colorful quality. Complete unanimity of feeling would after all bring terrific dullness. But reason is the quality which is obviously the same on both sides of the Rhine or the Atlantic, and at the equator as at the poles. Santayana had a phrase for it when he said, "We all move together when we pursue the truth." And I can never forget the remark of Professor Whitehead that reason has two sides—one Ulysses shares with the foxes, the other Plato shares with the gods. Of course reason can be used for scheming purposes and devoted to bad ends. But when people truly understand what it implies and what at its best it requires they will be lifted out of themselves into an awareness of the glory of the life it calls on them to share. That is why, as I say, I find ground for optimism in the growing faith in science and democracy. That is why also, as I shall try to show later, I believe that reason has its religious uses, that a passion for reason can become a passion for human brotherhood, and that education of the liberal type can have results for the moral as well as for the intellectual life.

Now you may see, he continued, why the fact that you caught me arguing against myself a few moments ago when we were discussing the kind of control ideas have over desires doesn't bother me at all. You will remember that in the old days in Athens we often used to change sides as the argument advanced. But we never lost our faith that there was a truth to be found if we could only get our terms clear and understand what they actually meant. Well, I believe that something like this faith is present in the hearts of many of our contemporaries today and that in liberalism, expressed through science and democracy, they have found that combination of a shared purpose with a tolerant acceptance of differences in individual details which will lead to unity in the long run. Of course we both wonder how long the run must be. A few more wars like this and there won't be anyone left to do the running. But am I not right in affirming that already we can see progress? For example, you made a real point when you said that the doctrines that have taken the liberal name arose in an individualistic age and are associated in the public mind with economic competition. But it is also a fact that today men are groping for an organic quality in experience and are trying to work out a more socialized interpretation than formerly. Remember also that liberalism had its Greens as well as its Lockes and its Adam Smiths. It seems inevitable that it should outgrow its individualistic stage.

After all, the liberal thinks of others as like himself, that is, as thoughtful people who are trying to be reasonable. Thus he lays the basis for coöperation and, although this may not be what the logicians call a sufficient condition, it is at least a necessary one.

Now that I've ventured into this personal area, he continued, and have started to comment on the human qualities of liberals and their opponents, let me make one more remark which, present company always accepted, seems to me to be long overdue. You have accused me and my kind of being dreamers with our heads in the clouds of generalized abstractions. I don't doubt there is some truth in the charge. But I think that many of my radical friends are lost in the muddy currents of the underworld of the unconscious. They aren't at peace with themselves or with anyone else. Much as I admire their courage and their readiness to respond to the challenge of action I sometimes wonder whether the action is well advised, and I'm bound to say that often they seem not to be well adjusted.

Isn't that in their favor? asked Simmias. Would you want men to be adjusted to a world at war or to be at ease in Zion at such a time? I think it is true, as you hint, that radicals pay more attention than do liberals to the darker forces of the mental underworld, but that is to their credit. They see and recognize them for what they are, whereas the liberal ignores them. And as I have indicated, a certain amount of maladjustment to the present world is highly desirable. Were the great prophets and reformers ever well adjusted to their immediate surroundings? The fact is that the vagueness in that word "adjustment" has caused a lot of trouble. Psychiatrists intended it to refer to a consistent ordering of personal interests, but the public has taken it to mean complacently harmonious relations with the contemporary environment, especially with its pleasanter, ice-cream and cake aspects. The personality well adjusted in this sense would accept the present on its own terms and would see nothing better to work for. An excellent example is the parasite. One difficulty with you liberals is that without meaning to you have really become parasites. Your eagerness for peace and for comfort has made you unwilling to face the facts of strife both in society and in yourselves. But the new psychology with its emphasis on power politics among unconscious desires helps us to see that the peace you liberals yearn for is an impossible state of affairs.

By this time they had wedged themselves into an elevated train and Simmias paused to catch his breath. A few minutes ago, said Cebes, you accused me of being wordy but you took a good many words to do it. You have also accused me of retreating into generalities, but it seems to me that your own indictment is rather general. The one empirical fact you have pointed to is the leave-takings in the railroad station. Can't you be more specific?

It's unlike you to ask for a bill of particulars, said Simmias, but I'll do my best.

I would find fault with both phases of the liberal's program, he began as the train started. The liberal is wrong in his treatment of both religion and education. In each case he has had ideas which were logical within their restricted sphere but irrelevant to actual life; in each case he has lacked a realistic program to which he could commit himself; while busy with his so-called ends and intrinsic values he has completely neglected the means that alone can give them significance. Just as this train is descending to the subway, so I think liberalism should come out of the empyrean and get down to empirical facts.

The elevated isn't exactly my idea of the empyrean, interrupted Cebes.

Let's begin with religion, Simmias continued. Liberalism intensifies religion's chronic faults of detachment and substitution of worship for work. No doubt the communists have ridden too hard the idea that it is an opiate. But I am still extremely suspicious of what is called the contemplative life and the genteel aids that it seems to require. When you sit in the luxurious surroundings of church, with your senses titillated by the beauty of music and architecture, can you truly claim that you are made more receptive to the social gospel, sometimes called the gospel according to St. Marx? No, the fact is that you are merely being confirmed in your hypocrisy. So many churches were built with money wrung from the hands of slaves. They may be called memorials but what they really memorialize is our human inability to establish justice. The God to whom they are dedicated is the Moloch demanding human victims, not the heavenly Father sought in righteousness and love.

Of course, Simmias continued, I'm not one of those who claim to know much about what goes on in God's mind or how he can be influenced by human appeals. But if I were to go to church at all it would not be to a liberal church. These criticisms from such men as Barth on the Protestant side and, let's say, Przywara on the Roman Catholic, have certainly hit the mark. If we take it upon ourselves to come into the presence of the great Creator of Heaven and earth and to call attention to our insignificant desires certainly it should be in an agony of self-abasement, far from the cool and confident, not to say calculating attitude of the liberal whose reason tells him just what to do and what to say, even to God. The liberal refuses to admit that he is merely a creature, dependent on God for everything good and especially for that greatest good, salvation. Christianity has a word for this refusal and the word is "sin." I am glad to see that sin is coming back into the best theological circles. The most profound religious truth is that man is judged not by his own reason, infected as it is with his ambitious pretensions, but by God's holy will.

Sin is coming back, he repeated, as can be seen in almost all religious literature. Instead of the smug belief in progress "onward and upward forever" our attention is turned to the sin of history. We are being made to realize that the perversions of history dog man's highest creative activities and frustrate all his seeming achievements. Progress leads only to perdition; technological advance to destruction. No one of us is free from the power of selfishness. Some of the greatest perils to democracy come from the fanaticism of moral idealists who are not aware of the corruption of self-interest in their own professed aims. A man may suppose that he is loyal to the common good but actually the claims of his family set him against his neighbor. As one writer with a gift for alliteration has put it: "Pure idealists underestimate the perennial power of particular and parochial loyalties." (Why didn't he say "purposes" and make the alliteration complete?) Reason itself has become not reasonable but a process of rationalizing, that is, a system of excuses for what our desires prompt us to do. If you doubt it, look around you at the advertisements in this car. Do they try to appeal to you as a reasonable being or do they, like so much else in our civilization, take it for granted that you are a suggestible automaton?

The worst sin of all, to which the liberal is peculiarly prone, continued Simmias, is the sin of pride and the worst pride is pride of intellect. Pride, seeking to hide the conditioned and finite character of all human endeavor, is, as so many writers today show, the quintessence of sin. The liberal considers himself a humble follower of the truth when actually he is a superb example of intellectual arrogance.

You remind me, said Cebes, of William James' story of the farmer who was called a rascal by a neighbor. He immediately smote the man saying, "I won't stand none of your diminutive epithets." Now I should like to suggest that you examine your own epithets, diminutive and other, and especially that epithet "proud." I doubt whether it means what you think it does. You will recall the Carmelite monk who said, "Yes, we may have to yield to the Dominicans in rationality, and to the Franciscans in piety, but [with sudden fire] in humility we can beat the world!" For my part I am wary of the pride of the dogmatist as much as of the intellectualist and I wonder whether the description of pride as infecting the whole human race isn't just another instance of the misuse of generalizations against which you have yourself protested so vigorously. If pride is characteristic of all human activity it is a meaningless idea. Furthermore if, as Calvinists appear to believe, God created the race with pride or knowing that it would succumb to pride, and now blames it for having this quality, he is a meaningless God. And as to this question of pride in the modern world, I must say that the most modern form of intellectualism doesn't seem to me to exhibit it.

The scientist is one who has developed a method of checks on his own prejudices which should make any pride he has ineffective. Thomas Henry Huxley said: "Sit down before fact as a little child, be prepared to give up every preconceived notion, follow humbly whithersoever and to whatever abysses nature leads, or you shall learn nothing." This does not strike me as a proud attitude, and while it is of course true that it describes the ideal rather than the common practice of all scientists, still it emphasizes the fact that the genius of science is in its ability to limit pride. The truth is that the word "pride" like the word "sin" has been distorted by our neo-orthodox theologians out of all recognizable meaning. They have looked around for a scapegoat in modern life and the phrase "sin of pride" came easily to hand. Actually our world is made up of some men who are diabolically selfish, others at the opposite pole who couldn't do a selfish act or show a vestige of pride if their lives depended on it, and in the middle a mass of struggling human beings like you and me who are sometimes selfish, sometimes decent, and always capable of becoming better.

So when I read all these modern books about the liberal's "hybris"—which, after all, isn't a modern word—and the smugness of his secularism and humanism, I wonder whether the charges are well founded. My own belief is that the liberal, in his eagerness to have his values well grounded and reasonably justified, has shown humility to a marked degree. Also I think even you will have to grant that he has won a fair share of freedom from the pride which is one of the worst of modern evils—I mean pride of class and sect. As I have said, the liberal is trying to find through his devotion to reason a basis for human brotherhood. He speaks for reasonable men not only of today but of all ages. You may remember the college boy who was asked to compare Herodotus as a historian with Thucydides. He replied that they were alike in many respects but Thucydides had the outstanding advantage of being alive at the time he was writing! Well, I think he was, and I think that particularly in the ideas he ascribed to Pericles he was alive to the issues of democracy in his own and all other times. Thucydides had the universality of the liberal mind, the mind that looks for the reasonable elements in his own age and in so doing appeals to reasonable men in all ages.

Still, you liberals fail to do justice to either the demonic or the creative emotions that govern men, said Simmias, especially as they appear in history. I once heard it said that the Germans believed that the history of philosophy unfolded with the express purpose of providing material for a textbook by Windelband. In the same way the liberal makes history too reasonable. He seems to think that when his mind is most truly logical it is most in accord with the processes of history and of nature as well. He misses not only the depths of tragedy and agony but the heights of loving emotion. The liberal is too fond of reason and too sure that it can always be applied. Accordingly he fails to do justice to the given datum, especially when it is a brute fact.

I don't see why this should be, responded Cebes. I think the reasonable man is simply the one who weaves as many data as possible into his consistent web. Some are not possible because they don't fit. In that case either they or the web must be discarded and a new start made. In a world full of give and take, not all the givens are taken because upon analysis not all turn out to have the proper credentials. But the ultimate test for any reasonable person must of course be that of coherence. The liberal merely hopes that in the presence of the given we can maintain an attitude of balance.

That's his mistake, for there is no such thing as balance in our society, replied Simmias as the train came to an abrupt stop, and he was pitched violently forward into the arms of a neighboring straphanger. The trouble with you liberals, he said as he recovered himself, is that you see poise and disinterestedness where there is none. Further, you generalize from particular instances of the given in an illegitimate way and you assign to general ideas a status they do not deserve. Now, as a pragmatic instrumentalist and a faithful follower of John Dewey, I object to your identification of abstract ideas with some higher form of reality. This is a tendency that you have carried over from the days when Plato distorted our master Socrates, and it is high time that you broke the habit. Untold harm has been done by the custom of setting up words like truth, goodness, beauty, honesty, and the like, speaking of them with bated breath, and then acting as if some especially virtuous deed had been performed by putting them on a pedestal. Let's understand, once and for all, goodness is what goodness does, for example to the unemployed, or better, to prevent unemployment. A student doesn't understand such words as goodness or truth until they are applied to specific situations. I myself don't understand the word gluttony until I ride my bicycle and discover what gluttony has done to me.

Further, I'm very doubtful whether you can assign any recognizable status to your general ideas because I doubt whether anything has existence except what is revealed in sense experience. When we say that something exists we mean that certain sensations come. In professional jargon a proposition is "factually significant" only if we know the sense observations which would lead us to accept it as true. Forgive me again for being technical in surroundings like these but I must point out that genuine propositions deal either with relations of ideas (in which case they are merely analytical and tautologous, signifying only our intention to use symbols in a certain way) or else they are empirical hypotheses which point to future sense experiences. The object of knowledge, like the result of a scientific experiment, is a sense experience in the future.

The evil of your method comes out, for example, when in your sentimental way you set up love as a general ideal which is itself an object of devotion. It didn't take modern psychology to show that love means all sorts of different things. My love for my country, for chopping trees, and for a good dinner have only the vaguest similarity. As for my love for you, that is the most completely unexplained, not to say unreasonable quality in all experience. Consider the value of love in one of its concrete meanings, namely marriage. In our present world the value itself is distorted. First, marriage is postponed by the unsettled times, later it is thwarted, unless the young couple has enough income to keep up with the Joneses. In other words the meaning of the value itself depends on social and economic circumstances and can't be known apart from them.

As to the future status of the object of knowledge, I can explain that by referring to our present journey to Cambridge. Thinking enters into this experience so far as we are practically purposeful and have something to do after we get there. At present Cambridge is the goal of our thought. You may say, as has been said before, that Cambridge is but a state of mind, yet the important fact is that it is a future state of mind, a prospective reference, as Dewey would say. Boston, of course, is merely prior or antecedent reality, that is, something either to transform or to get away from as fast as possible. There was, as we all know, the Boston lady who would not travel because she was there already. Now Boston, as you see, was antecedently real to her in such a way as to block the prospective and future reference which thinking should have. It is only by getting away from this loyalty to static ideals and prior absolutes and discovering the selective and purposeful nature of thought that we shall make progress.

You're already getting way ahead of me, said Cebes. I would still maintain that some conceptions have an intrinsic meaning, apart from their practical usefulness, and that some resist your empirical tests and wither away before them instead of yielding up their meaning to them alone. Consider democracy, for example. It means: Persons are equal. Where are the observable terms in this proposition? A person as a self—a thinking, willing, feeling being—is not observable, even though his body and external behavior may be. "Equal" in the proposition doesn't mean anything that you can see. It signifies not equality in size but in rights. Carry the argument one step further. Can your type of empiricism say what we mean by rights? A right is not a phenomenon that is observed here and now but an ideal or value that ought to be observed and derives its significance from its claim. It is a demand on our behavior, not an object that we can sense.

As usual, said Simmias, you've gone at the problem from the wrong end. Democracy points to something very concrete for it means the application of democratic procedures to social life. To say "persons are equal" is to express a proposition that acts as what we call a motivator and tells us how human beings ought to be treated. Do you say that a value is unobservable? What you mean is that a value as a motivator is observable in and justified only by its consequences.

Here the train stopped at Park Street and, before they could converse further, both Simmias and Cebes were carried out the door by the mad scramble of their fellow passengers. It's lucky our purposes were in line with those of our immediate environment, Cebes managed to murmur as they rushed downstairs and boarded a train for Cambridge. The last I heard, he said as they caught their breath, was your defense of instrumentalism. But didn't you feel a certain instability in your own position as you were carried out the door? You may recall the occasion when Mark Twain was an instrumentalist. During one of the Mississippi floods he and a friend were perched on the furniture awaiting the oncoming waters. As the room filled, the friend floated out the window on a table while Mark accompanied him on the piano.

Oh, well, said Simmias, if you want to treat serious matters as a joke, go ahead.

No, replied Cebes, I'm only making a pun and you will agree that for Freud a pun represents one of the higher associative processes of thought. I'm also enjoying a smile, and even Dewey allows us this type of consummatory experience once in a while.

Yes, but in your case it was anti-social and irresponsible, said Simmias, if you were really trying to bring me around to your view. And that leads me, he continued, to my criticism of your neglect of social forces and influences in general. After all, I can use the illustration of our being carried out the door with as much point, probably more, than you. I would take it to show that neither a person nor an idea can be torn out of its social context without doing it violence and forcing it to lose its meaning. When the great social revolution comes we'll understand this readily enough. Just as we were swept out of the door by the urgency, economic and patriotic, of the desires of our fellow passengers on their way to the various factories, so society will soon rise in its wrath and sweep out of its way the astigmatic thinkers who are trying to keep their attention fixed on abstract problems. The forces we face are those of coercion, not cajolery, and he who stands idly by talking of reasonable devotion to detached truth and of indifference to social purposes will soon find society supremely indifferent to the purposes he himself has.

Before you go further, said Cebes, let me say just a word about some of these ideas you have picked up from Professor Dewey. I have always wondered at Dewey's insistence that the object of knowledge is in the future, as the result of an experiment, because I don't see how the experiment is to be carried on unless you already know the data you're dealing with and the methods you're going to use. In that case aren't the present circumstances actual objects of knowledge? Further, Dewey's blast at general rules seems to me to be highly colored by partisan feeling. What of the general rule that there are no general rules? In Dewey's own philosophy is there any situation where the experimental method or creative intelligence should not be used? Is there *any* exception to the use of democratic procedures and coöperative measures? Dewey's philosophy is itself full of general rules.

You said you were going to attack the liberal theory of education, he went on. Please be sure you first understand

what it is. I would refer you to Cardinal Newman's arguments
for liberalism in his *Idea of a University*. Newman points to
the kind of knowledge that is worth having for what it is
rather than for what it does. Knowledge is one thing, virtue
another. For my part I think I see what he meant. The intellectual life has its own demands and comes on its own
terms. If our students think that ideas and facts exist only to
be applied to their own purposes, no matter how worthy or
how social the purposes may be, they miss the point of the
quest for truth and dull the edge of their mental sensitiveness.
You remember Charles Peirce's remark that he belonged to
that class of scalawags who prefer, with God's help, to look
truth in the face, whether doing so be conducive to the interests of society or not.

Yet Peirce was the first of the pragmatists, answered Simmias, and for him the real meaning of ideas was in their consequences. As for Newman—you couldn't have chosen a
better example for my argument. Read that essay of Newman's again and you'll see that for him the liberal is the
gentleman who doesn't soil his hands with servile work.
Indeed, that's what the idea has meant ever since our discussions in ancient Athens, and the tragedy of it is that until
the war our liberal arts colleges, unconsciously perhaps, main-
tained the tradition of liberalism as a tradition of indolence.
College students aren't hewers of wood or drawers of water.

Drawers of pictures, then, perhaps? interposed Cebes.

Our students maintain or try to maintain the genteel tradition, continued Simmias, ignoring him, while others do the
work of the world. The liberal arts college is a leisure-class
conception. But the time is not far distant when it will have to
justify itself to those who make the leisure possible.

Is that the best interpretation of liberal? asked Cebes. My Oxford Dictionary defines liberal arts as those worthy of a free man, opposed to servile or mechanical. This doesn't mean that the free man is opposed to the mechanic. There was no thought of mechanic or of slave either. The idea is that a free man by virtue of his freedom has a certain dignity and that the arts appropriate to him are those where this freedom can find expression.

Of course there was no thought of slave or mechanic, answered Simmias. That's just the trouble. Our definition makers like our educators have acted as if the working class didn't exist. But, unconscious though it may have been, the effect of their activity has been to keep down the worker and to keep up the old class loyalties. Oh, I don't mean loyalty to the Class of 1916, but to the class that the critics of our late President used to say he betrayed. You think that liberalism in education means open-mindedness. Don't you see that in our economic system open-mindedness is impossible? Education must be for the worker or against him, and it may be most effectively trampling on his rights when it supposes itself to be most impartial. The class struggle is a more serious matter than the freshman-sophomore tug of war, and it is time that our colleges woke up to their part in it.

Every time you begin the old story about the warfare between the classes, said Cebes, I have to remind you that what your New York friends call the Marxist ideology doesn't apply in this country today and didn't apply even before the war. The classes have merged, laborers are stockholders, our students represent all income brackets and many of our professors have both white collars and membership cards in the A. F. of L. You don't help your own argument by stressing this fact of class conflict. We feed the fires of such conflict as there is by talking about it so much, and we prevent our students from taking the impartial view that the search for truth requires. Further, you accuse me of making idle if not vicious generalizations. But you yourself make one that affects and distorts all your thought.

What is that? asked Simmias.

Why, said Cebes, following Dewey you take the social as the most inclusive category. In fact Dewey somewhere has an essay with that title. For him the social includes all other ways of describing life, such as the mechanistic or the vital, and because it is so inclusive he thinks it is all-important. Furthermore he seems to think that it alone helps us to understand what value means. Now it seems to me that there are values—artistic, intellectual, and contemplative—which need not be social in his sense and need not, as the pragmatists claim, point to any future experience. For example, what of Wordsworth's emotion recollected in tranquillity? What of the mathematician's formula? Perhaps it has to be socially confirmed before it is put to work, though even this is doubtful, but certainly its validity doesn't depend on the number of people who agree that it is true. For the mathematician "a to the zero power" equals one, though a majority of our fellow passengers in this car or even of the fellow members of our society and perhaps even you and I can't really understand what that means. No, I hold that man is as truly a logical as he is a social or political animal, and that where truth or rightness or validity are concerned he appeals to certain logical norms that are absolute in the sense that they exist in sublime independence of what society thinks, though the life of society may well depend on what they are. Society itself must correct its judgments by the appeal to logic. With your final reference to the standards of the crowd you are like the passengers of this car in that you leave no room for the individual. As a matter of fact, the theorists who appeal merely to the social milieu are as provincial as the research scientists who can see no intellectual method but that of the laboratory.

The hobgoblin called consistency doesn't haunt you very closely, does he? asked Simmias. First you call my ideas too general, and then too provincial. But it's your armchair college professor who really hails from the provinces. He retires to the tower lined on his behalf with solid ivory—though, as others have remarked, today it has become a sort of cyclone cellar—and starts talking, of all things, about what he calls reality. The fact is that he lives in a dream world and doesn't wake up till reality comes along and pinches him. When classes fall off and his salary is threatened he begins to suggest dropping the Latin requirement and introducing vocational courses. Like the rest of us, he doesn't really think until forced to by a practical emergency. The only way to get him aroused is to make him see the social forces that actually direct his thinking and then hope that when he sees them he will try to control them. The professor in his provincialism is like the Californian who defined America as California and a few outlying states. "Don't be too sure," said the New Englander when he heard it. "No other state could outlie California!" In other words, an exaggerated enthusiasm for one's own interests is likely to reflect a very limited outlook.

There was once a German professor's wife, remarked Cebes, who observed that twenty-five years ago her husband's lecture hall was filled but that now no one came. And the thing she couldn't understand, she said, was that the lectures were exactly the same, word for word, and comma for comma, as they were twenty-five years before. Now I am forced to say again that I have heard these phrases about social conditioning for about twenty-five years and they are beginning to sound a bit stale. Of course a person is receptive to social influences when he rides in a car like this one, reeking with democracy and filled with an unmistakable social atmosphere. But if the philosopher would only come with me to my camp on the Belgrade Lakes and watch the light on the water in the morning and the gleam of the stars at night he would see that the natural environment is both more elemental and more inescapable than the social, and he would talk more about the methods a person uses to put himself *en rapport* with his natural environment—to understand it, to use it, and at times simply to contemplate it in awe. Nature has various ways of calling to us. Sometimes it speaks to us through our dumb but powerful emotions of wonder and the sense of mystery. Sometimes it seems to ask for loving sympathy and adoration. Sometimes it needs to be understood in detail and used for the right purposes, and then we get out our microscopes or our logarithm tables. It may help and strengthen us to have companions but I find it hard to think that, except for the particular kind of knowledge called scientific, the presence of the companions is the essential and determining factor. And of course I hold that we know other things than physical nature; for example, there is knowledge of values. That is why I balk at all this reference to the social category as final and authoritative.

What therefore, he continued, you call my passion for universals comes merely from an irresistible feeling I have that certain distinctively intellectual processes a man goes through as an individual offer him the real basis for discovering both truth and goodness. One of these processes is that of forming general conceptions and assigning to them a status that your empirical particulars do not have. Another is that of drawing logical conclusions. Now like you I view philosophical idealism with some suspicion. For example, it appears to me that the orderliness of nature is of a mechanical rather than a reasonable type. But this does not prevent me from recognizing that the presence of mind in human life is, after all, the most overwhelming fact we confront. The two extreme procedures are either to expand one's view of the world to take account of mind, as in philosophical idealism, or to reduce mind to the level of physical nature, as in naturalism. I admit the dangers in the inflation of idealism and am unwilling to go all the way with the idealists. But reducing at the wrong times and in too violent a manner also has its drawbacks. It seems to me that with your constant reference to social categories you are like the Freudians in reducing mind *ad libitum,* which really means *ad libidinem,* even when you talk of social good, for your social goods resolve themselves into economic goods or objects of crude desire. You tend to think this way, as I say, because you live in overcrowded Washington and are so constantly in the midst of swarms of people. Why, even Dewey was an Hegelian idealist when he lived in Vermont. It was only when he moved to Chicago, and later New York, that he changed his views.

But the point, said Simmias, is that one can understand the individual, his knowledge and his values, only in his social relations. Therefore the whole problem should be viewed in the light of its social setting. You can't have the right kind of education, for example, without providing the correct type of association with others. Personality is adequately developed only in certain special forms of community life. Society sets the problem and suggests the terms in which it must be answered. There is no such thing as the detachment you profess. There is no thinking-in-vacuo even in a head like yours. Thinking occurs only in response to social situations. Now what I want to emphasize is that in these the forces of intrenched power and prejudice are ever active. Our colleges are bound, consciously or unconsciously, to reflect the point of view of their supporting groups. Let's be aware of the danger, then, and face it.

This is where you play right into my hands, said Cebes, for in so far as it involves judgment the process of facing the danger is carried on by the individual in abstraction from his fellows. You just spoke of the risk of being influenced by group loyalties. Would you say that the only way to resist it is to play one group off against another or to accept the views of the group that wins in the long run? The real question, of course, is how you define winning and what you mean by the long run. I believe that we should seek the truth as individuals before we try to apply it in society. So far as education is concerned, naturally I want our students to have a mature social point of view. But I am primarily eager to train them to make judicial decisions, which will apply to this or any other society in which they may happen to live. We are moving toward collectivism today. But it is possible that in the world of tomorrow collectivism will have to be curbed and the area of individual appreciation emphasized anew. As to philosophy—I agree that it has been pretty remote and that it might conceivably be better in the present emergency if all philosophers, perhaps with the exception of the very great ones, should quit philosophy and get into the fight. But if they should do this I hope they would have the sense and decency to call themselves practical warriors or practical social reformers rather than philosophers. Whether for good or evil, philosophy and practical activity are not the same thing. If we're going to have philosophy at all we must take it on its own terms and play the game.

For you it seems to be only a game, replied Simmias. It is like a crossword puzzle, except that you use the same old words without looking up new ones. At that moment the train came to an abrupt stop at Harvard Square and Simmias trod violently on the toes of an elderly gentleman reading his morning newspaper.

It is as I feared, remarked Cebes. Like the man in Galsworthy's play, your care for society has made you lose sight of the individual. As we leave this crowded car, let's remember that while some find safety in numbers, others find it in exodus. Before we part I want simply to indicate the kind of exodus education and religion share. You have talked about liberal religion as an escape. I think that religion, especially of the liberal sort, is not an escape but a legitimate withdrawal. It helps us to take the longer view, to find relief from worrying details, and to see life whole. Education should do the same. Yet of course it would be fatal if either religion or education should mean final evasion of responsibility. Both should bring renewal of our energy for fighting. Antæus received this from Mother Earth. Arjuna in the *Bhagavad Gita* gained strength for combat from detachment. The mount of vision and the active healing of the demoniac boy are parts of the same picture, as Raphael knew. Mary and Martha have complementary roles to play. The intellectual or moral absolute in its detachment and perfection is not a refuge for the weak but a challenge to the strong and a sign of that by which he conquers. Its requirements are not such as to make it sought by the lazy mind.

The two friends mounted the stairs quietly, Cebes in a meditative mood, Simmias still somewhat combative. As they emerged into the rain of Harvard Square Simmias narrowly escaped a truck that was trying to pass the light before it changed. They used to burn heretics with oil, he said. Now it is simpler to run them down with gasoline. But heresy will win in the future as it has in the past.

Yes, said Cebes, but heresy wins because its ideas are true, and I doubt if one can say that they are true only in so far as it wins. Of course truth is not completely isolated. It is the truth about the facts of our experience. Obviously it must be relevant to the forces in the individual heart and in society. The question is—of what sort is this relevance? The forces you speak of are ruthless but they are also objective. They play no favorites. There was objectivity even in that truck, you know. It aimed for me as well as for you. It rains on the just and on the unjust, but a little more on the just, because the unjust has the just's umbrella. Now reason can't get in the way of trucks and hope not to be run down, or of rain and hope not to catch cold. But, knowing the dependability of both trucks and rain, it can devise its own means of controlling one and diverting the other. In this process it has to cultivate a kind of judicious detachment, a sort of indifference to special wants and desires which for the moment and for this particular purpose sets it above and apart from the rest of life.

Look at the matter this way, if you will. Both in society and in the human heart there are two levels of experience.

One is that of nature, the other that of reason. If you ask whether reason isn't part of nature I have to answer that while in one sense everything is part of nature, in another, and more significant sense, reason is separate. Nature is the home of mechanical forces, operating sometimes in organic relationships, but still in an impersonal and deterministic way. When you have reason, however, something new has been added. Reason is free to choose the good motive, the relevant fact, the consistent idea. I don't see such freedom anywhere else. Now of course this freedom is circumscribed by more factors than we have time to discuss at present. Yet it is not squeezed out entirely and the amazing fact that it is here and operative at all is what has attracted the liberal and furnished the basis for his philosophy.

The question how a man is to meet these impersonal forces that surround him becomes, therefore, the question how he can transform mechanical into reasonable necessity. The latter cannot operate in a vacuum, of course. Reason needs nature, though nature often works in independence of reason. But when nature is transformed by reason and brought under the control of coherent ideas, then and only then do value and significance make their appearance. You have said much about the blind and even demonic forces in the human heart and in society by which we are controlled, and you are right in reminding us of their presence. But if we recognize them exclusively and forget that it is our constant duty to transform them we miss all the possibilities the higher life has for us. With the growth of this so-called realistic trend, he went on, and this eagerness to meet force with force and to pay attention to the sordid as well as the serene, I fear the rise of a philosophy and a practical attitude of expediency. Of course reason is not always effective. Does that make it the less reasonable? Of course justice is not done; does that mean we should not seek it? Of course truth is forever on the scaffold— is not love also forever on the Cross?

Let's not forget, he continued, that reasonable and liberal methods demonstrate their relevance sometimes in the most unexpected places. Reports from the front show that combat units are more powerful in battle when they are organized along democratic lines. I'm told also that mental breakdowns are fewer among those fliers who are brought up on liberal ideas, in the sense that they know what they are fighting for, as contrasted with those who fly for the sheer thrill of adventure. Democracy itself may develop weaknesses in times of peace, but look at its magnificent strength, unity, and purposefulness in war. What has been called the new belief in the common man bids fair to become a force that will sweep many of the older institutions out of its way. The search for truth itself is far from the pallid, cold, and unemotional activity you have made it. Actually it requires courage, sympathy, persistence, discipline, and devotion of a high order.

As to your claim that liberalism makes no appeal to youth, he continued, I want you to remember that for years our enemies tried to make people believe that democracy was outworn and that fascism alone was a creed fit for young men of vigor. But as a matter of fact it is despotism and authoritarianism of whatever sort that is ancient and democracy that is perpetually renewed by the youthful energies to which it appeals. Some day, God willing, we shall visit again that remarkable Reformation Monument at Geneva and thrill once more to its resounding phrases honoring the ideals of liberty, equality, fraternity, and the right of man to act in accordance with his conscience and reason. And let's not forget that the liberal gospel comes to us not merely from the Europe of a special period but that it represents the universal demand of the human spirit for autonomy and that this is as old as civilized man and as wide as the world itself. Democracy is its political expression and those who oppose liberalism today should take care lest they find themselves opposing democracy tomorrow.

Later, he said as they continued to walk up Brattle Street, I want to apply this to the special problems of religion and education. Just now, before we part, let me call your attention to the peculiar fact, hard as it is for us to understand, that you and I need each other, and that this may be because the dualism of life and idea that we have mentioned may have its productive side. I am eager to analyze ideas dispassionately and to find out what they really mean. With your vigorous social conscience you can help me to see that ideas must be put to work if either their inner meaning or their outward application is to be made clear. I am much concerned for the cultural disciplines in education, you for the vocational. I would say with Royce that an idea is useful because true, you with James that its usefulness is a clue to its truth. I want society benefited by a passion for learning, you want learning pointed up through its social application. I want a religion that allows me to see the world in the light of the eternal because I think that is the true light. You want a religion that focuses on present need because that for you is the relevant fact. What we should understand is that both sides of experience are important and that each can respect and profit by the other's insights without being false to his own. But what's this? he asked, stopping short.

Nothing but the house of Longfellow, a mere nineteenth-century liberal, said Simmias.

No, I mean the building across the street, said Cebes. There's a hint of the solution. That is the Friends' meeting-house. The Friends believe, as you will recall, in the absoluteness of the inner light and in the uncompromising nature of the search for truth. Yet what group has been more active on behalf of society? These people have formed the vanguard of the movement to free the slaves, to crush the liquor traffic, to emancipate women, and to eliminate war. They show that the ideal need not be idle. In fact, they make me think that together we form an Hegelian synthesis.

I'd rather say that it takes both you and me to make a world, said Simmias, and the two friends parted.

II

THE LIBERAL DEFENDS A DYNAMIC RELIGION

ON THE second lap of their trip to New Haven, Simmias and Cebes occupy a seat in the coach of a train running from Boston to Providence. Although they are still aware of a surrounding cloud of witnesses they do not feel that the claims of society are so pressing or immediate as during the ride in the subway. In leisurely fashion they settle down to talk about what religion is and does.

———————

We were discussing the role of ideas in a world seemingly ruled by impersonal forces, said Cebes, and I gained last time the impression you were not wholly sure that it was by ideas or by the liberal's use of them that the world would be saved.

The remark does justice to your academic caution, replied Simmias. I should prefer to say that the appeal to reason, as a method and a philosophy, is all washed up.

Hobhouse once remarked, said Cebes, that although great changes are not caused by ideas alone, they do not come without ideas. I wonder whether you aren't a little confused as to the role that ideas and reason may be expected to play. Admitting the justice of much you have said and trying to use your own approach, I would still hold that the appeal to ideas and the attempt to keep them coherent is a basic human interest.

I want to try to make clear the role of reason in religion, he continued, because this is crucial for my whole point of view. We both agree that man's need is desperate. You say the need will be met by a glorious God of majesty. But who is this king of glory? The old answer, shouted by conquering armies massed at the temple gate, their spears still dripping with blood, was: "Jahweh of hosts, the Lord mighty in battle." Yet I think that the writer came nearer to the truth a few verses earlier when he said that the man who may ascend to the hill of the Lord is the one who has clean hands and a pure heart. If God is really an object of worship, and if he is to act as God in human experience, he must be a God who knows what cleanness means. This is to say that he must be a God for whom values are of primary importance and his own power must be of the sort that values can exert. Now the liberal is the one who best understands what this signifies because, as I shall try to show, he has the right approach to a knowledge of what values are and how they work. Let me put the matter in this way. Religion is devoted and loyal commitment to the best that reason and insight can discover. The liberal understands what loyalty to the best means as the authoritarian never can.

On the contrary, almost any form of authoritarianism would seem to me more religious, said Simmias. Take the Roman Church, for instance. It has a dignified history, a supernational organization, a well-articulated philosophy, and a ritual that symbolizes in unparalleled form the cosmic drama of creation and regeneration. Further, in such devices as the confessional it shows that it understands what goes on in the human soul. Or, if you wish a tradition nearer your special background, take Calvinism. It has its own majesty and grandeur in its theory of the Sovereign Creator and Ruler of the world. And surely recent events have verified its low opinion of man.

So often I hear Calvinism praised by men of your type, broke in Cebes rather irritably. Yet I don't see that you go on to join and attend the Presbyterian Church. This is what we *would* believe, you say, *if* we believed anything. Well, who is dreamy now? I'd like to ask. Who is playing with ideas and allowing them to be artificial instead of forcing them to meet the issues of life? As to its pretensions to authority—of course Calvinism claims to speak for God. But the same claim has been made by thousands of others who turned out to be false prophets. You spoke of its majesty and grandeur. Yet what do you mean except that, by your own confessedly fallible standards and in your own eyes, the Calvinistic God appears to be a Superior Being? The truth is that you simply can't escape the judgments of human reason and appreciation in religion or elsewhere. You may recall the old lady who at the age of eighty took up the study of Hebrew. When her friends asked why, she said it was so that she could talk to God in his own language! As a matter of fact, God has to talk our language if we are to understand him, and if we don't understand him I see no use in talking either with him or about him. But if he talks in language that we understand he must talk in terms that are reasonable.

Don't you believe in revelation, then? asked Simmias.

Let me ask you this, said Cebes in reply. How do you know a revelation when you meet one?

Probably by its uniquely overpowering character, said Simmias.

Yet the psychopathic hospitals are full of people who have accepted revelations on that basis, said Cebes. My strong feeling that I am right does not make me right, nor, I regret to say, does yours justify you. There is a distinction, my friend, between psychological certitude and reasonable certainty, and too often it turns out to be the distinction between delusion and truth. Of course I'm not saying that every datum that insists powerfully on being heard must be false. I'm simply affirming that every datum, whether it comes forcefully or feebly, must be interpreted before we can know whether or not to accept it as true. As it comes it makes a knowledge claim. It is not actual knowledge until we have submitted it to the tests of coherence and found it to conform to fact and to be consistent with the rest of our reasonably established judgments. Every sense experience, value experience, or experience of God must be put through the critical mill, must so to speak become liberalized and, in a good sense, rationalized, before it can take its place in the reasonable stream of thought.

Even the man who deliberately rejects this process makes use of it according to his lights, Cebes continued. The man who says "I have a revelation straight from God independent of my reasoning powers" is using his reasoning powers to accept the experience and label it revelation. In his own limited way he is reasonable and critical in spite of himself. This is why I just cannot understand my erstwhile liberal friends who have now gone over into neo-orthodoxy. They have had a taste of the liberal method and they know how inescapable it is, yet they pretend that they can by-pass it. In the defense of their orthodoxy they actually use all the liberal arguments. This belief fits the facts of history, they say—it works well in human experience and is consistent with the best that human thought has produced, including the latest speculations of Eddington and Millikan. How they can affirm this in one breath and then go on in the next to talk of the complete unknowableness of God is what I cannot understand. The old Scotchman was more forthright who said, "Nay, it isna guid, it isna recht, but it is the will of God!"

What about neo-Thomism? asked Simmias.

As I just indicated, replied Cebes, if we are careful about what we say we can't call both neo-Calvinism and neo-Thomism true. The reason is that they differ in their statements as to the medium for God's grace. Many of my neo-orthodox friends try to gloss over this difference as if they were not aware of their own lapse into a tolerant liberalism in doing so. Others, somewhat like the modern Calvin-lovers, appear to me to play with Thomism and to make believe that they can adopt its philosophy without actually joining the Roman Church. This I hold to be dishonest. If Catholicism is true, accept it; if not, then don't. Or if we are to take the tolerant position that truth in religion sometimes eludes exact creedal statement we should do it on the basis of a frank acceptance of the liberal's confidence in freedom of thought and an equally frank rejection of arbitrary institutional authority. A man once remarked to an Anglican friend of mine, "I suppose you think the Episcopal church offers the only road to salvation." "No," replied my friend, "but I will say it offers the only road a gentleman would wish to travel." You can't have it both ways. Either you think, as the authoritarians do, that your road is God's and all others lead to perdition, or, with the liberal, you believe that because of differences in background, training, or temperament men may travel different roads and yet reach a common destination. In this case you hold that the varieties of religious experience may express a common truth in differing forms.

To modify the figure, he went on, the liberal in a sense believes that there is an only road to salvation but it is a much wider and much more traveled road than that of his authoritarian friend. Entrance to it is based on tests that are not creedal but moral and reasonable. Neo-Thomism seems to me especially dangerous at this point. I have known many neo-Thomists who were as surely headed for salvation as anyone who ever lived, but as persons they seemed to me to transcend their official beliefs. Officially they would be forced to exclude certain would-be fellow travelers not merely from their own road but from any road at all. As two modern neo-Thomist writers have put it: "No state is justified in supporting error or in according error the same recognition as truth." * Yet who is to judge what is error? God, of course. And who knows what God judges to be error? Well, who indeed, if not the person or institution to whom the truth has been specially revealed?

This, after all, he continued, is one of the crucial problems of our day: How shall we treat error? I will merely remind you that in a regime with truly democratic procedures I may believe that my neighbor is in error but so long as my welfare or that of others is not threatened I have no right to suppress

* J. A. Ryan and F. J. Boland, *Catholic Principles of Politics,* p. 314, quoted by Reinhold Niebuhr, *The Children of Light and the Children of Darkness,* p. 127.

him. If, however, I am an authoritarian and live in a country which the authoritarians in their special phrase call "organically" theirs, his suppression becomes not merely a right but a religious duty. For an authoritarian church other sects exist by favor. For the liberal, an authoritarian church itself exists by right until it begins to deny rights to others. Consider also the fact that although questions of faith, where the church's decisions are binding, are supposed to be kept separate from secular questions, the two fields often overlap. Who shall judge, for example, whether birth control is a religious or secular question and whether all citizens shall have access to relevant medical information? Further, how can a strongly authoritarian church ever accept any new truth which would force it to admit that it had made mistakes in the past? But I think that the basic trouble with authoritarianism, especially in times like these when society is already falling apart, is that it injects the notion of partisanship into what should be non-partisan. Of course there is a point where the liberal himself must take sides and must fight for his own cause. But I have less fear of his intolerance than that of others because he adopts intolerance for tolerance's sake.

I still don't think that you have answered the criticism that liberal religion lacks the authority of God, said Simmias.

How do you suppose God makes his will known? asked Cebes in reply. Do you really believe, as some of these neo-orthodox pretend they do, that the qualities of wrath and vengeance should be emphasized? Do you really think God is like a jealous master with a slave? The trouble is that so often one slave enjoys the idleness and another slave receives the flogging. Is it in accordance with your ideas of God's justice that our generation should allow a greedy economic system to grow up before our eyes and that our sons should pay the penalty with their lives in war? Or do you really think that a Creator as such has authority over both the lives and the consciences of his creatures? Tell me, why should the act of creation yield authority? What moral or reasonable loyalty does the creature owe the one who, without his will, created him? I do not think the issue is made easier by the claim of the neo-orthodox that God must be a Creator who stands above history if he is to redeem it. In fact I don't know what their kind of redemption can mean, either in history or above it. I don't see what now or later can redeem the bestiality of the present moment. Let's face this clearly. No real redemption, in the old sense, is possible. *We* can't bring back the life lost nor undo the moral injury nor relieve more than the smallest part of the suffering in the world today. And even *Heaven* has no balm that can really make it good. But we under Heaven can go on from here to make the shattered fragments form at least a piecemeal pattern and we can find worth in doing so. God as a Creator and Redeemer above history therefore seems to me irrelevant to the moral problem. The creature may bend to the Creator's will, but being bent this way is not religion as I understand it. Man is a reed, the weakest in nature; he is a bent reed and a broken one; but it is the fact that he is a thinking reed that gives him his religion along with his other higher experiences. We are workers together with God, not slaves driven to a task in which we have no heart and for which we have no mind. To return to our earlier definition: Religion is active, devoted, and loyal commitment to the best that we can discover, and the best can be discovered only by using our reason for all that it is worth. Religion goes beyond ethics in its moods of devotion and its assertion of our dependence on a good, greater than ourselves, at work in t.. world. It goes beyond the analytical procedures of reason in the romantic quality of its surrender to the ideal. But it is at one with both ethics and reason where the claims of either are relevant. On this account I think of the essence of religion as loyalty to the rational good.

Wasn't it Heine, asked Simmias, who said that God made man in his own image and that man was quick to return the compliment? You're falling into the old liberal vice of making God conform to your standards. If there is one thing that seems to me sure about religion it is that it is a relation where God judges man, not where man judges God.

Heine was wrong, said Cebes, and so was Xenophanes, with his talk of a fair-haired God for Thracians and one who was snub-nosed for Ethiopians, in so far as he thought that the effort to make God intelligible makes him less than divine. No one, with the possible exception of the most primitive savage, ever made God in his own image. To say that God must be reasonable is not to say that he must conform to any man-made standards. When man listens to reason he listens to a voice that comes from a plane above his natural life. And a God of goodness, by the definition itself, is one who far transcends human achievement. No man is good as God is. Even the best man, and perhaps he especially, hungers and thirsts for a goodness that is ever beyond him. It is characteristic of goodness to be dissatisfied with present accomplishment. Further, so far as judgment on man is concerned, I should like to know what can more adequately pronounce judgment on human activity than the principle of reason itself.

Nevertheless, said Simmias, I miss the overpoweringly dynamic note of the Lord of Creation in your account of the divine. I often recall the impatience of the professor of theology who said in class: "Don't let me ever hear again the dirty little word 'values.'" I must say I sympathized with him. The emphasis on values in the current liberal trend would rob God of his dignity and power.

On the contrary, said Cebes, I think it tries to understand what his dignity is like. I too remember that remark of the professor and I know that I wanted to cry out: Prithee why so hot, little man? Why get so excited over what seems to you like an effort to demean God when God, by whatever definition, is so far above all of us that to demean him is out of the question? Even if the professor disagreed with the approach through values he should have taken more pains to see what was involved. Men have turned to values because they furnished the surest possible refuge from the prevailing winds of doubt. This is the real motive back of the value philosophy. I sometimes wonder if its opponents understand how strong the forces of skepticism are in this bewildered age. But where Descartes said he doubted all except his own process of doubting, others have found it more helpful to say that in the process of doubting, the standards of honest thought cannot themselves be doubted. We cannot doubt the distinction between better and worse. This has been an anchor to windward for many an honest mind. Whatever happens these values remain, and the fact that they have to be interpreted and applied and fitted into practical and specific situations does not alter the abiding quality they have as abstractions.

Now surely, he continued, it is one of the tasks of religion to point to what is abiding in this sense and to give men an object of loyalty of this type. This, I think, is what Arthur

Clutton Brock meant when he said that if there is a God he must be according to our values. When he went on to say that our values are not merely ours, and that they are far from having been invented but are rather discovered by us, he showed how completely beside the point is the type of criticism you are making. I know that in your effort to indicate how God must be exalted above such things as values you will quote Tersteegen at me and will say "Ein begriffener Gott ist kein Gott." In reply I can only say that quite literally when you utter those words you do not know what you are talking about. The liberal does at least use language people can understand.

Even if you are right, replied Simmias, and, mind you, I'm not at all sure that you are, the liberal is still wrong in his intellectual approach both to values and to God. The experience of doubt is a highly specialized luxury indulged in by the philosopher and few others. The type of salvation you describe may appeal to some but I can't believe it is a very large or very important group. When I think of the history of religion with its color and pageantry, its wrestlings with the spirit, its agony and abasement, its complete abandonment in sacrifice, its triumphant conquests and its lifetimes of loyal devotion, your pallid abstractions seem irrelevant and remote. The philosopher may have a prominent place in your kind of heaven, but most people, myself included, would put above him the saint, the mystic, the prophet, the martyr, or even and perhaps especially the humble and penitent publican.

If I give the impression that philosophy alone is worth while, said Cebes, I am seriously misstating my own case. I don't want all men to be philosophers, much less to be professors of philosophy. For one thing they would have to support themselves not by taking in one another's washing but by teaching one another's children, which would be just as disastrous.

At present all they do is to hang out one another's dirty linen, muttered Simmias.

Of course I believe the man in the street might well cultivate his more philosophical interests, Cebes went on, just as I think the philosopher might well spend less time in his study and more in the market place. He would then understand his neighbor more sympathetically and would have a better idea of how to go about solving the most important problem of the times, which is: how to live more amicably with those around us. But what I want to emphasize here is that religion should provide us with an object of loyalty, that we can be truly and wholeheartedly loyal only to what we see is of worth, and that the question what is ultimately of worth can be settled for the inquiring mind only by a process of abstraction where the critical intelligence is brought into play. Of course religion is not all intellectual; in actual experience it is not even primarily intellectual, since in its essence it is an emotional attitude of loyalty. But what seems to me not to be always recognized is that the emotion itself depends for its validity on a rigorous analytical process, and that the analysis must be made by someone. This is where the philosopher comes in.

Naturally, he continued, I don't mean to say that only a philosopher can be religious. The man with no interest in philosophy who devotes himself to the cause of love, worships it, and patterns his life by it, may be much more successfully religious than the one who is more articulate in his explanation of just what goes on. But I want to emphasize that the basis of God's claim is one with the claim of truth. God's claim is broader, of course, because it includes other values, such as justice, love, and beauty; but the way God's demands act on us can be seen most readily in the truth situation. The liberal is the one who understands the pervasiveness of this claim of reason. It is he also who exposes it to view and explains its nature. Indeed, that is just what we are trying to do in this very conversation. We are analyzing ideas and testing their coherence. Right now it is more appropriate for us to do this than to start singing "Keep your hand upon the throttle and your eye upon the rail," even though the passengers might be edified by such a duet, or to ask the good-looking Yale alumnus across the aisle if he is a Christian. Like President Timothy Dwight in the well-known story he would probably think we asked if he came from Princeton! Besides, the answer to such a question is bound to be relative, whereas strictly logical analysis takes us into the realm of the absolute.

I suspected the worst, replied Simmias, and now you have realized my fears. Back of all that talk about reason I felt sure the shape of the absolute was lurking. In my view the absolutist is public enemy number one. Any absolutist depends on intuitions which are notoriously untrustworthy, as you yourself hinted in your discussion of revelation. Your own intuitions make you as bad as Hitler; in fact worse, because you ought to know better. Where are your checks and controls? Where are your ways of finding out what the absolute really means in daily life? The absolute may be useful for the lecture on metaphysics, but when you come home afterward, and the children throng around to ask how to spell a word or do a sum or to prevail on you to help them with their roller skates you'll quickly forget the absolute in the presence of all the relatives.

The chief difficulty with the word "absolute," said Cebes, is that it has unfortunate connotations. Yet if we reject it, we shall have to find another to express the unquestionable authority God has over us as the rational good. Religion, I have said, is based on loyalty to the highest we know. Through the highest, God makes a claim on us. For our present inquiry I think this claim and its character stand out more significantly than the equally obvious fact that God saves us. There is no question about our need to be saved but there is plenty of room for honest questioning as to how our salvation is accomplished. Theologians have had a perfect field day in their attempts to describe it, but the net result of all their speculations is not one of those clear and simple truths that all minds can grasp. Now it seems to me that if there is a God, and if he does save, the method of his salvation should be of a sort that all can understand. And I think that the normal healthy mind and conscience does grasp the claim of the higher life. I think, also, that religion becomes intelligible when we identify the claim of the higher life and its values with that of God as it does in no other way. If you would worship the gods, the old Stoics used to say, imitate their perfection. It doesn't take a philosopher to understand that kind of teaching.

When I talk about absolutism in religion, therefore, what I have in mind is the compulsory quality in the value which must needs be accepted by the normal human being. You see its nature most clearly when you see how reason works. For example, you can't deny reason without affirming it; you can't argue against it without presupposing it. Even though

we don't always obey its rules, reason itself is inescapably
there as a set of standards for our thought and conduct. We
sometimes sing a hymn which bids us check the rising doubt
as an influence that may interfere with our faith in God. But
if the doubt is honest, would God have us check it? It seems
to me that the presence of doubt in an inquiring mind may be
one of the surest signs of God's influence. Don't you see that
although the two do not completely overlap there just can't
be any conflict between faithful search for truth and faithful
service of God? Don't you see also that altogether too much
of the time we describe religion in terms which make such a
conflict inevitable?

You have spoken of the arid and barren quality of a religion of reason. Two comments should be made here. The
first is that the effort to find truth and to apply it as justice in
human relations ought to be the most thrilling and colorful
activity open to us. It ought to make God's presence as real
and as compelling as any means of approach that can be of-
fered. It draws on all the nobler emotions. It requires not only
insight and discrimination, but courage, loyalty, and loving
devotion of the highest order. Beyond this, it gives us a share
in a crusade as broad as the life of humanity itself. It makes
us participants in an enterprise which has no sectarian ambi-
tions but has enlisted the best energies of men of integrity
and good will of every age and every clime. The second
comment is implied in what I have already said. Truth is a
value but not an exclusive value. It does not rule out the
others, such as justice, love, and beauty, but it entails them.
Reason insists on being applied as justice and in being loved
as beauty. Plotinus put this in philosophical terms but in

doing so he expressed an insight common to philosophers and non-philosophers alike.

It appears to me, therefore, Cebes continued, that the liberal's interest in reasonable values is of a deeply religious sort. It offers loyalty that is absolute in the sense that it cannot be questioned by the honest mind; it brings the exaltation that can be found only in dedication to the highest; it binds all men together in a common purpose. In these troublous days I have often wondered, he added, whether the growing prestige of the idea of democracy does not stem from the fact that men are beginning to sense their need for a concept that stands for what is universal in political life just as reason stands for what is universal in thought. A reflective person is devoted to democracy not merely because it gives him more freedom but because, in theory at least, it breaks down all barriers and gives every man a chance. What we chiefly abhor in fascism is its exclusiveness. The issue is joined today between those beliefs and methods, like democracy and science, which emphasize the common qualities in experience and the various particularistic irrationalisms which pander to the interests of special groups.

This is why I believe in following always the hints that reason gives us and I have less and less sympathy for attempts to set religion and reason at odds with each other. As a former pupil of Socrates it should not be hard for you to understand one important way in which reason plays into religion's hands. As I have hinted before, reason is a universal discipline not only in that it calls on all men to use the same methods of thought and not only because, especially in science, it gives each fact equal weight, but also because it treats a fact always in the same way. It establishes generalizations or symbols of uniformities in experience. It sets them apart as abstract ideas and points to some of them, like justice and temperance, as objects of devotion in their own right. This was Plato's interpretation of the world of forms and I think it is not hard to see both its basis in reason and its relevance to religion.

Worse and more of it, grumbled Simmias. First you confront me with absolutes and then with generalizations which are just as bad. Generalizations are a refuge for the shirker, diverting his attention from the specific jobs to be done. The day will come when, as Dewey has prophesied, men will be ashamed of their devotion to general rules and proud only of their awareness of specific facts and their means of dealing with them.

Yet certainly you can't apply justice to the particular case unless you have some idea of what it is you are trying to apply, said Cebes. The notion of justice should at least act as a pointer, indicating the direction to take, before you can begin to behave like a just man. As Plato showed, the abstract notion of justice is a generalization but it is also something else. It is a limit to a series, an ideal to which our experience is a mere approximation. Now surely it is this superiority in value rather than superiority of power that distinguishes the divine from the human. A world that contains such values in their transcendence of all that humanity can hope to achieve is a world with religious quality. The limit stands above the series of approximations but, so far from being irrelevant to them, it is what gives them their significance. My opponents seem to think that they have played a trump card when they ask where these ideal values are. Well, when so many thinkers far abler than I have disagreed on where to place them I don't feel that I can offer a worth-while solution for this knotty problem. But certainly it is true that they exist in so far as they are actualized in the thought and behavior of human beings. At least they are also possibilities for experience, standards for experience, and in the moral and esthetic life it is a psychological fact that they act as stimuli to experience. Each of us would be hard put to it to describe completely the metaphysical status of the perfect circle or the ideal notion of equality, yet each of us uses them in his thinking.

Such illustrations may have held for our talk in former days in Athens, said Simmias, but modern science has made them irrelevant today. Jeans has shown, for example, that in the minute world of the atom or the gigantic world of the nebula the familiar statements don't hold. The sum of the angles of a triangle is 180 degrees only so long as the triangle is not of either astronomical size on the one hand or sub-atomic on the other.

Yet, said Cebes, the mind that compares the three triangles obeys one set of rules of logic. Jeans finds a way of bringing all three into one intelligible universe of discourse. Whatever new subtleties of perception and measurement may have been introduced for these new fields of research, the conceptions back of them are still in common use by all rational minds.

I'd rather say that we still find certain conceptions useful instruments in the process of knowing, said Simmias. These abstractions are convenient fictions, but they don't have the status you give them. Indeed, the more abstract and pure they become, the more they "transcend," as you call it, actual life, the less value do they have. When you say, for example, that justice is a value or has value, you mean that there is value in just acts; when you call health a value you mean that it is a good working condition for actual living organisms. For special logical purposes you can separate "value" from human behavior, but when you do, the "value" itself disappears. When you talk of truth as an ideal you really mean that knowledge of true facts is helpful in the actual struggle to get along. Justice is good because our society couldn't survive unless men developed the habit of doing right by their neighbors. Men want that kind of society—this is why justice can be called a value. Worst of all, your talk of ideal justice and beauty inflates your ego and gives you the pleasant illusion that talk alone will bring justice to pass. It is an irresponsible form of self-indulgence cultivated by sentimentalists who want the rewards of idealism without its penalties.

To his surprise Simmias found that Cebes' face was gradually assuming a bright crimson hue.

Come, come, he said at once, you know I'm not personal in this. I mean only that for idealists in general the right to praise ideals must be earned.

Unfortunately your criticism strikes home altogether too pointedly, replied Cebes; it applies with painful exactness to me and to many like me. It would be a fine thing if I could have you constantly at my elbow to jog my conscience. At the same time, I think I can help you to see life more steadily, instead of swinging so violently as you have in recent months from extreme pacifism to extreme militarism, from a tremendous enthusiasm for liberal arts education to a desire to put the colleges all at once at the service of the war effort, and from a convinced atheism to the place where you're not sure whether you ought to join the ranks of the neo-orthodox. As to the changes in conceptions and their application, let me point out that food remains food and toxic acid harmful even though, as George S. Kaufman rather inelegantly said, one man's Mede is another man's Persian. Justice does not change because men are unjust; truth remains an ideal in spite of the lies of this war; friendship is friendship even though my friend betray me or I him. Of course I have to grant that there is real danger in the frequent repetition of words like justice and truth and I must agree that some speakers who use them make me think of nothing so much as a juggler tossing toy balloons into the air; still, when appealed to on the right occasion, they bring strength and not weakness.

After all, he continued, value resides essentially in the reasonably established good and in conceptions like justice which have their place in a coherent scheme of ideas, rather than in objects of interest which owe their supposed status to fleeting and even crude desires of the moment. I know you would say that an object in order to become a value needs only to be desired. I believe, however, that it should be fit to be desired. And I think that we are aware of its fitness only after we have compared it with other desires and other requirements and have judged it worthy to take its place among those we have set up as ends for our conduct. To say "I want it" is to express a passing impulse. To say "This is good" is to make a judgment which places the impulse in our consistent scheme of accepted goods. Value thus requires the appeal to reason. An act or an object is not made a value by the fact that it is wanted. When the assassin desires the murder of the good man that does not make the murder a value, even to the assassin. And of course the question whether justice is a value merely because it has worked well in history I can an-swer only in one way. I believe justice is a value because we know, reasonably, that just acts are always good, and we can-not imagine a case where they should not be performed. Thus, if you push me, I should have to say that I believe justice and truth would be values even if they had never worked well, though, since they are what they are, I admit it is difficult to describe a society where they could never work well, or where they would be valued as justice and truth if they had not. In the last resort I suppose I should be driven to say that where they do not work well there is something wrong with the society rather than with them.

But this brings me back to the main issue which is that the intellect in carrying through this process of abstracting values uncovers the authority resident in the generalization as such. A general idea lays down a requirement for the mind. The fact or quality or rule to which it refers has to be treated by all minds in the same way each time it is met. When the generalization expresses an ideal or a limit for active effort, as in the case of justice, it stakes out a claim and exerts a lure for the moral as well as the intellectual life. Rightly taken, it re-veals a new dimension of experience—the dimension of those objects of attention that appear with a dignity and authority of their own as ends in themselves rather than as means to any selfish purpose whatever. The vision comes most convinc-ingly in the case of the truth and its obvious claim upon us, irrespective of what our own wishes may be. It is made more clear as man reflects on the varied rules of reason and their manifold demands on him.

For the moral life, he continued, has two parts: seeing what to do, and doing it. It is true that ideas can't be permitted to exist separately. They mustn't be allowed to remain abstractions but they must be taken as such first of all if we are to see them truly. Further, if we really see them as they are I think they will not stay separate very long. Plato, who argued for them more eloquently than anyone else, didn't leave them apart, you will recall. Instead of merely pleading for courage, temperance, and religion he wrote a biography of a brave man facing death, a temperate man meeting the pleasures of the banquet, a religious man praying under the plane tree. Nevertheless I think Plato held that Socrates was what he was because the values were what they were. And for my part I think this is where the emphasis should be placed even though I admit that there is a practical sense in which you can say that the values were what they were because Socrates was who he was.

Today, he went on, we find new intellectual methods of which Athens had no comprehension, and they throw new light on the nature of the moral problem. For example, the liberal stands for tolerance, a moral quality, and coöperation, still more clearly a moral quality. But where, in our modern world, do we have a better example of coöperation than in the distinctive contribution to intellectual methods made by modern times? What is science but the triumph of coöperation? Today to be an intellectualist doesn't mean to be a dreamer but to be one of a number of experimentalists concentrating on working out a common problem. The intellectualist in these times is a participant in a great coöperative enterprise who sets us a moral example at the same time that he presents us with new facts. Thus today the revolt against the intellect as a refuge of the bystander has lost its point. We don't need to rebel against the mind in order to stress the will. We don't have to revolt against philosophy in order to be socially minded. We aren't compelled to come down from the clouds in order to be active in the market place because our best thinkers are no longer in the clouds.

This development, he continued, seems to me to be a part of the natural unfolding of the moral and practical qualities latent in the life of reason, and I think the liberal is the one who has sensed its inevitability. As we have just noted, it all started back in Athens when the person who dealt with the things of the mind found that he had discovered the moral implications of intellectual law. He felt the moral requirement laid down by the general idea. He sensed the control which the predicate as an abstraction exercised over the concrete subject. In the syllogism he became aware of the compulsions of entailment and inference and as he reached further into the realm of speculation he learned about the binding force of the laws of coherence. Furthermore he began to love some of these general ideas like justice and truth with a devotion we can only call religious in its absolutistic quality. He learned to regard them as representatives of another world than that of the give and take of daily life. He saw that the kingdom of ends required him constantly to give and didn't make any promises about what he would receive. Also, he began to see the moral virtues of the imagination which as it generalizes reaches out for analogies and tries to free itself from slavish literalism. Today the development of the scientific method helps him to conserve these gains and also to have a hard-headed aggressiveness and an ability to deal with practical, tangible material that he lacked in the past.

Furthermore, he continued, I want to be sure that you see one of the great advantages of liberalism, which is that it saves us from what has always been the besetting sin of the narrower religions and what bids fair to be the final threat to civilization itself—I mean the attitude of parochialism. Surely if it did nothing else this awful war should have opened our eyes to the horrible danger of immersing ourselves in our own immediate tribal prejudices. The liberal with his passion for what is universal at least makes an effort to get away from them. But it appears to me that the neo-orthodox trend has the effect of renewing these creedal barriers in all their exclusiveness. In what seems almost a willful way it insists on bringing out the particularistic features of Christianity. It emphasizes the special revelation vouchsafed to those lucky enough to live in certain places at certain times. It goes on to anathematize the poor liberal who is merely trying to hint that perhaps other traditions had their own ways of approaching the mind of God. Many of the neo-orthodox try to revive the partisan issues raised by the Reformers, who were, indeed, great men for their time, but who undoubtedly would not express their ideas in the same way if they were alive today.

No, said Cebes, warming to his subject, I believe we should not be limited to any century: the sixteenth, the thirteenth, or even the first. Truth comes out of all of them, and we found a great deal of truth under our own master in the fourth century B.C. I have lived long enough in non-Christian lands, he went on, to know that other cultures have their profoundly spiritual conceptions and their deeply significant insights. What is more, I would join hands with my Jewish neighbor and my Buddhist brother today to say that the deepest truths outstrip any theological framework whatever and to affirm that a Kingdom of Heaven that has anything else than tests for admission that are moral and, in the best sense, spiritual is no Kingdom for which I have any concern. Let me join rather the Republic of Truth or the Democracy of Brotherhood.

You still haven't progressed far from your besetting vice of dealing in glittering generalities, said Simmias. All of us want to join the Republic of Truth and the Democracy of Brotherhood. The question is how.

Yes, that is at least one very real question, said Cebes. But it will not be answered by stressing denominational differences. What I crave, both now and for the period after the war when men will be full of the spirit of revenge, is a common creed in which all of truly good will can share. This gives me sympathy with the religious humanists who deny God but make so much of social unity. The difficulty there again is that, like the orthodox themselves, they seem to glory in what they don't have. Just as the orthodox take an almost gleeful delight in man's sinfulness and his inability to save himself, so the humanists are practically ecstatic over the view that there is no God. Why shouldn't both be more positive? Let the humanist continue to set forth in his own persuasive way the unlimited possibilities that will be open to us when the day of brotherhood shall dawn, and let the orthodox stress the incalculable benefits of faith in a God of love. Then let us all try to see how naturally one supplements the other.

Before you go further, said Simmias, I want to point out that you still have failed to meet two crucial objections. The first is that although you have talked glibly about the parochialism of your opponents it is actually the liberal who is tied to a special spot in time and space without realizing it. The liberal treats his generalities as if he could really abstract himself from his own private prejudices. Actually each general idea is infected with the provincialism of petty desires, and the liberal is worse off than most men because he continues to shut his eyes to this fact. Secondly, although of course you do not admit it, you are really a humanist of the worst sort—worst because you pretend to be something else. You try to raise yourself by your own bootstraps while, speaking in all reverence, you fail to see the latchets you are unworthy to unloose.

On the first point, said Cebes, I would say that the liberal at least makes an effort to get away from his limitations while his opponent seems to take the fetters of a special place in history as something to be proud of. On the second I would say that so far from relying on human ideas I am actually trying to listen to the voice of God through the only channels by which it can speak. Can God communicate with us except through reason and conscience? Of course the element of mystery is important in religion, but isn't it the mystery which arouses wonder and interest and curiosity and which in the end stimulates our sensitiveness to value, rather than the mystery of the unknowable? God is not to be defined by his sheer difference from man. This to me is meaningless. God is other-than-man-in-achievement-of-value, greater than man as the ideal is greater than imperfect accomplishment. Also he is greater as the source of value must be greater than any human and finite experience of value.

> Wer Wissenschaft und Kunst besitzt
> Hat auch Religion;
> Wer jene beiden nicht besitzt
> Der habe Religion.

Goethe was right in that there is a sense in which he who has science and art has religion, although not necessarily in its completeness. If he doesn't have them, he needs religion; if he does, he needs only to follow their implications through to find religion as loyalty to God, the source of our values.

Nevertheless, said Simmias, your eloquence should not be allowed to obscure the fact that where values are really being produced and where work of the sort you really want done is being done it is by groups devoted not to values in the abstract but to a religious faith based on a particular creed and rooted in a historical tradition. In Germany the real resisters were not the liberal professors but the members of the orthodox churches. In England are there any more truly forward-looking people than the members of various Christian sects? Here at home I don't know where more important planning for reconstruction is carried on than by earnest Christians who are trying to meet practical social issues with intelligence coupled with prayerful devotion and the Christian spirit of sacrifice.

I agree to what you say about the work now done by Christian groups, said Cebes. I believe in these groups, and I don't want to see them go over into neo-orthodoxy. But I believe in them because they meet the liberal's test. They seem to receive a special stimulus from the fact that they belong to a particular historic tradition, but their work is reasonable and good by any liberal criterion. My only plea is that while we keep this membership and this connection we stress always its liberal side, realizing that for the most part what the church does is good but not thinking that it is necessarily good because the church does it. Even today, I regret to say, some church groups have a rather limited view of how to think of the new heaven or to plan for the new earth. It is true that liberal breadth should draw on orthodox depth but while the orthodox does the prodding, the test of what is good is in the liberal's standard of reasonable value.

The orthodox is the only one who feels the stimulus provided by the tragedy of history, said Simmias.

Do you mean to say that you are taken in by that kind of statement? asked Cebes. People like Kierkegaard and Barth constantly claim that they alone do justice to tragedy in all its bitterness. Actually I think that they are trying to exploit this fact of tragedy, the most powerful element in the thought of every sensitive person, for their own special purposes. Further, I think the measure of their own awareness of the tragic side of life can be seen in the terms they make with it. They turn from tragedy to find refuge in a Creator God as if they didn't see that a beneficent Creator becomes more inexplicable than ever. A God who created the world we have today doesn't fit very easily into the role of an object of worship. I don't think the situation is relieved by saying that man's freedom is responsible. In the first place, this ignores the unimaginable amount of animal pain which must have occurred before man and his freedom appeared on the scene at all. Second, if God is an omniscient Creator he must have foreseen this evil and at least connived at it. Third, I think even our finite intelligences can imagine the outlines of a world where freedom would not entail such disastrous consequences in agony, viciousness, and cruelty as we see today. For my part, I recoil in horror from the traditional idea of a God who in his wisdom and power foresaw what was coming, created the conditions for it, and now expects our thanks and praise. We must modify our ideas of religion because of these facts to stress value rather than power, and if we do we are using our reason in a liberal way.

It is strange to hear you as a liberal talking in this fashion, said Simmias. It is the liberal who, blinded by his optimistic confidence, has always shut the door on the stark facts of tragedy. It is the liberal who has irresponsibly tossed about such words as righteousness and justice as if they could be made to apply to the world we know. The war, we say, is waged for justice, but is there justice for the men in the front lines who do the waging? Is it just that boys of eighteen who have not yet known the joys of love, marriage, and parenthood, or of having a productive job of their own, should be asked to kill and die so that two aging verbalists like you and me should have a chance to discuss justice peacefully on our way to New Haven? It's a wonder the word doesn't burn our tongues as we pronounce it! James once wrote of the intolerable state of a world where men had their happiness at the expense of one poor suffering wretch condemned to a life of torment. But millions today are meeting experiences that will send them to hospitals for the blind and the insane and the incapacitated for the rest of their natural existence. Is freedom for us worth this price for them? Yet, in the course of the evolutionary process, has not freedom for the leisured few always been bought at the price of the suffering of the many? Sometimes, like Ivan in *The Brothers Karamazov,* I feel like saying that I want to give back my entrance ticket, since life on these conditions is intolerable.

For a while after Simmias' outburst Cebes looked out of the window in silence. Finally he remarked, in a quiet tone of voice: We passed the village of Sharon a short time ago. It reminded me of the Plain of Sharon I once crossed in Palestine and the Plain of Esdraelon adjoining it. The Sharon Plain was part of the great military highway from Syria to Egypt. Over it passed the armies of Thothmes, Rameses, Sennacherib, Cambyses, Alexander, Pompey, Titus, Saladin, Napoleon, and other famous generals of history. Deborah sang about the way the hosts of Barak swept down from Mount Tabor to the Plain of Esdraelon to overwhelm the Canaanitish army under Sisera. You will recall that she claimed that the stars in their courses fought. When I looked down from Nazareth on the great plain I wondered whether many of those who struggled there must not have felt that men were bound to fight in their courses as the stars in theirs, with no relief until the end of time. The renewal of war today forces our generation to ask the same question. Yet as I stood there I caught sight of an orphanage set up by our own Near East Relief, and I remembered that this association had saved, at a conservative estimate, a million lives.

Now a million saved is not so many compared with all that have been lost, but it suggested to me that at least we should not dismiss ideas and ideals as wholly ineffective. From the hill of Nazareth two thousand years ago an influence had gone forth across the plain, had traveled around the world, and had returned finally to bring hope and healing to this plain itself. Its idea of love and brotherhood has been forced to compete with the lust for power, property, and prestige, and much of the time it has waged a losing fight. But it is still there, above the struggle, a rational good, worthy of the utmost devotion. In spite of the fact that it is frequently obscured by the clouds of passion and desire, I don't see what else is so worthy or what has more right to our allegiance. The question whether it balances the awful suffering of men and animals is unanswerable because meaningless. Luckily we don't have to answer it unless we insist on taking a rigidly orthodox view. The question we *are* asked is what we can do here and now to put that idea to work, and we are furnished with a clue to the answer in the symbol of the Cross which stands for the suffering that love requires.

With much of what you say I agree, said Simmias, but I must point out that you have given your case away in saying it. When you affirm, for example, that the question about the worth-whileness of life as a whole is meaningless, you point to the limits of liberalism. Some questions probe too deep for reason. That is what I have been trying to suggest all along. The world is unreasonable in the sense that it doesn't give us what we want. On a deeper level it is also unreasonable in that it does not give the just man what he wants in his most disinterested and reflective moments. He can't find satisfaction when he thinks of the tragedy around him. Thus the sensitive man can live only by perpetually blacking out what would take away his peace. Reason has a very small area in which to work. Furthermore, such thinking as we do about the worth of life depends primarily not on reasonable considerations but on the given and fixed conditions under which each individual life operates. It is the givenness and unrecallableness and finality of the fact that we have been placed here without having been asked whether we wanted to be that determines what we think about life. This is probably what people have in mind when they emphasize the worship of God as Creator. I think this is really what brings urgency to our moral strivings. Further, it dictates to reason by forcing the decision that life is good, since thought realizes its ultimate dependence on life and is unable to deny the goodness of its own sustainer.

I believe, he continued, this is why religion, seeking in a practical way to meet the fact of tragedy, arouses the active energies and appeals to the more elemental springs of conduct instead of raising the speculative question. Philosophical like financial speculation seems to gain life from a rise in the stock market. But in a crisis it gives way to something deeper. At such times, when you with your arguments might suppose the problem of evil would make any thought of God impossible, religion appears actually to flourish. This is because it opens vistas ordinarily closed and taps springs ordinarily hidden. We know at such times that the question "Why?" is not the deepest question but that our dumb and inarticulate yearnings must seek satisfaction on some profounder level.

To your appeal to thought I would therefore oppose an appeal to life, and I think mine is more fundamental. It poses the question, and on final issues it dictates the answer. The energies of life lead us on to their own conclusions; the satisfaction of the desires of life provides the setting even for the intellectual problem. Today the liberal himself must see that we need a more dynamic motive and a more practical criterion than the one he offers. For example, the fact of survival enters into the determination of the nature of values themselves. What would have happened to the values of liberalism and democracy if we had lost the war?

I can't believe, said Cebes, that they would be lost forever, even though the setback is too terrible for us to contemplate. But the really important question is not our survival but the survival of the cause of democracy. In other words, it isn't survival as such that is the test. I agree that your appeal to life should be made and I agree also that the problem of evil is so overpowering that no final reconciliation on the plane of thought is possible. Of course one could become a materialistic naturalist, and then this problem would not arise; but others would appear, including the problem of good. Even so it seems to me that we should not give up the effort to find reconciliation. "If I held truth captive in my hand," said Malebranche, "I should open my hand and let it fly, in order that I might pursue and capture it." Truth, in other words, is on the wing. Reason, likewise, is a continuous process just as much as it is a formal scheme of ideas. Truth is that which we are given the privilege of trying to find. On rare occasions we do find it and, with the possible exception of certain obscure questions concerning the worth of life, we find it most surely by abstracting ourselves as well as our ideas from the urgencies and the needs for decisive action that you make so prominent. Furthermore, in places where the head gives way to the heart I believe the head must itself see why it does so.

Each of us has a tendency to become one-sided, he continued, which we must try to correct. I don't want a two-faced philosophy, nor have I been drawn to the figure in the *Theologia Germanica* of the two eyes of the soul, because it always seemed as though they might work at cross-purposes. But it takes only half an eye to see that life and thought must each make its distinctive contribution. And I do not mean to speak in too much of a partisan mood, he went on, if I say that, when they unite, thought should have the last word. You will recall that Plato used to appeal to a myth when he wanted us to see old issues in a new light. Let me try to express what I mean by an illustration from music.

That will be giving life the last word, said Simmias. As Nietzsche pointed out, music suggests the flux of Dionysos rather than the calm of Apollonian thought.

Certainly it does justice to life, replied Cebes, but I think one can show that both life and music lend themselves to treatment by thought. Let's take the emotional Tschaikowsky as representing life and Beethoven in his more classical mood as suggesting the formal canons of reason. Now consider the contrasting ways in which they dealt with tragedy in the *Pathétique* and *Eroica* symphonies respectively. You will recall the theme of the *Pathétique*. Mi re do la sol, mi sol do-o-o la sol, he hummed, somewhat brazenly. What superlatively beautiful music it is and how agonizing at the same time! But it is art and not metaphysics.

What an advantage! said Simmias. Isn't that just what Tschaikowsky intended?

It may be, said Cebes, but when you raise the problem of tragedy, as you yourself intimated some moments ago, you should go on to point to some kind of an answer. Life itself will not allow us to leave it hanging in mid-air or in the middle of the scale. This music goes round and round but, so to say, it doesn't come out anywhere. It is the music of a mood that finds no relief. It writhes and wallows in its own agony, asking, like Clarence Day's father, "Why did this have to happen to *me*, to *me?*" and finding no answer.

But Beethoven from the start suggests the formal structure of ideas rather than the vagaries of individual feeling. Do mi do, sol do mi sol do, he begins in forthright fashion on the cellos, giving you at once the chord of the scale he plans to use. Then in the middle of the first movement he works up to a series of dissonant crashes, using strings and wind instruments with alternate strokes, for all the world as if to represent man beating in agony on the door of his prison house of tragedy and demanding in desperation that he be released. But almost immediately, with no change in harmonic structure, the music resolves the difficulty and proceeds on its melodic course. Man has found the way out. How? Simply by realizing the significance of form and the function of universal ideas. Beethoven has shown this not only by the use of formal chords but by appealing frequently to the percussion instruments. It is as if he were taking us out of ourselves and our private feelings by beating in bronze a pattern which is like an idea that all can see and share and understand. In this case the idea is that the prison house is the realm of cause and effect. Tragedy comes because we live in an orderly world that plays no favorites but strikes down all who get in its way. But Beethoven shows that cause and effect are necessary for the dependable environment in which alone mind can feel at home. Because our world is regular we can have science, art, habit, character, morals—all that makes life worth while, even religion itself. And it is mind dealing with dependable material that does this, working upon causal necessity, as we saw in our last conversation, to change it into reasonable necessity, and facing tragedy in the only way it can be faced, by seeing it as a part of the larger network of relations of which good, and especially future good, is also a part.

Providence! came the voice of the conductor at this point, breaking in on their conversation. Simmias and Cebes reached for their belongings promptly and started down the aisle. That's why I can't think of Providence as merely a sudden interruption of the causal chain, said Cebes, but rather as a reasonable outcome to certain of our hopes and plans where mind has been in control. Furthermore, I never come to the city of Providence without thinking of Roger Williams. He was a liberal who lived in the world of ideas, yet did not neglect the active work of practical reform. But I think the genius of liberalism has changed between his time and the present just as it has between our life in Athens and our life now. In Roger Williams' day liberals were forced to separate from the majority to establish a new frontier. In their turn they became orthodox and saw new minorities move away. Today it seems to me that the genius of liberalism and democracy is not separative but unitive. The new frontiers of our world are to be found and tamed not by proclaiming a division within humanity but by seeing its essential unity and devising procedures which will bring this unity to the fore. That is one reason why freedom in our time must be interpreted in economic as well as political terms. The economic problems of the world community must be solved before any freedom worth the name is possible. But this should not daunt the man who believes that reason is a positive force in human affairs.

Simmias made no comment and the two friends descended into the station tunnel. The mechanical train of cars and the reasonable train of thought were both left behind.

THE LIBERAL EXPOUNDS HIS VIEWS ON EDUCATION

Wᴇ have a fine day for our talk about liberal education, remarked Cebes, as the two friends drove out to the Providence airport on the last lap of their trip to New Haven. How appropriate, replied Simmias, since liberalism is so clearly a fair-weather view. Just in case this should be our last ride together, he added, eyeing with some apprehension a few clouds on the horizon, I want to explain that my objections to liberalism come sharply to focus where education is concerned. I am convinced that liberalism in education means social irresponsibility. Years ago, when people believed that nature was at work automatically to produce better men in a better society, there may have been some excuse for keeping intellectual and social interests separate. Everyone thought that in a world governed by reason all would come out well in the end, no matter what the colleges taught. But recently a great deal of water has passed over the dam and some of our most cherished social institutions have been nearly swept away. Democracy has escaped destruction in war at the hands of its external enemies only by the narrowest of margins. The question now is whether it can resist its internal enemies in time of so-called peace. If two world wars in one lifetime can't make even the most detached liberal feel the threatening conflicts in our society and the need for facing up to them in all our teaching, then I fear he must be given up as hopeless. Selfish forces are at work to which even the most isolated classroom cannot remain indifferent. The real question is whether the good earth and its products shall be developed for the benefit of all men or exploited for the profit of those with the shrewdness and skill to keep others away. It is time for professors themselves to stand up and be counted in for one side or the other if their professions of disinterestedness aren't to be counted out entirely.

I've never denied that the liberal should take sides on a moral issue, said Cebes, and I hope I haven't implied that liberal education is morally neutral. I've merely tried to point out that truth-seeking is a distinctive enterprise with a special set of rules of its own. When we are engaged in it we should not take sides too quickly. Nor should we allow the search itself to be defined in terms of practical purposes unless we see clearly that the word "practical" has in this case a more inclusive meaning than ordinarily. I've also said that we easily lose sight of what the truth is if we keep asking what it should do here or there or what side it should be on. That question we raise as moral men rather than in our special capacity as truth-seekers. I admit of course that the distinction is a delicate one and may be pressed too far. Perhaps the whole issue between us comes from our disagreement about just where to stop. But it seems to me that you tend to ignore the distinction altogether and that in so doing you run the risk of erasing truth from the list of human goals. Whatever you put in its place may be important but it will not be the same.

Now of course you are right when you say that we have had a terribly rude awakening and that we have been shocked to see how near the apparently placid surface of the stream of life are the destructive forces of violence. But to me this suggests how significant are the spheres of non-violence that remain and how essential it is that education shall keep our eyes fixed on the decencies of peace. Even though we have had to copy the methods of the fascists by appealing to arms, I am happy to think that for the most part we have done it without glorifying arms and without losing our conviction that the resort to violence is justified only under the most extreme provocation. It behooves us today more than ever to explore the ends and methods of peace and to see what neglected sources of power they may have. One way is to allow liberal education to devote itself to the goals of reason and to follow them with complete loyalty.

I just want to remind you, interrupted Simmias, that the word "reason" is now held in suspicion as never before. We are aware today not only of the tensions in society but of the crafty forces at work in the unconscious life of each person. Much that used to go by the name of reason is known to be sheer excuse-making or rationalization. You have heard a philosopher defined as a blind man in a dark room looking for a black cat that isn't there. Perhaps you have heard also that a theologian is a blind man in a dark room looking for a black cat that isn't there—and he finds it! Today our neo-orthodox theologians, working with the psychologists, have found the black cat—several of them in fact—in the dark underground caverns of the subconscious. They see that our professions of reasonable disinterestedness are tainted by ambition and by a kind of pride we just can't escape so long as we remain in an unregenerate state. At bottom we simply don't want to live as reasonable beings. Therefore the man who talks about reason as an educational goal is prejudiced in a way that has dire social results.

You have talked a great deal about my prejudices, replied Cebes, and about my limited knowledge of human nature. Yet I cannot help believing that your own point of view is less subtle than mine and takes fewer facts into account. You are profoundly disturbed by the world's evil, as indeed you should be, and you want to attack it immediately. This makes you eager for a religion where power is at a premium and reason is less important. It makes you yearn likewise for a kind of education that takes its place at once on the side of the forces of righteousness. My position is that these moral and social ends are sometimes won by a flanking movement that includes more territory because its method of advance is less direct. For example, I cannot feel that a religion that is out of line with reason will maintain its appeal in the long run. I understand, of course, that any religion must and should arouse powerful emotional loyalties, but if its basic structure is not founded on reason it will not endure.

With education the case is similar. Human nature, we sometimes say, is too subtle for any argument, but it is also too subtle to dispense with argument. It will not always respond immediately to reasonable persuasion, but it will not long be satisfied with any attempt to by-pass the methods of persuasion. The difficulty, I think, comes from our faulty recognition of the exact role reason plays. As I see it, reason, like all absolutes, has to be treated with a deference that is both steadfast and flexible if it is not to be lost altogether. I mean that it is one of those peculiarly baffling goals which are nonetheless necessary because elusive. It forces us to give it a place apart if it is to remain with us. It has to be set on a sort of pedestal if it is to influence what goes on around the pedestal. As some would say, you must aim at the absolute if you are to hit the right kind of relative. Or, as others have put it, with more elegance, life presents us with a rhythmic alternation where we seek the detachment of disinterested truth in order to return with discernment and power to our attachments. The mystic has found this to be the case in religion. I think the liberal is the one who sees it most clearly where education is concerned. The truth is useful but if we seek it primarily for its immediate usefulness we miss it. That is why liberal education (*a*) must define its aims in terms of abstract reason and truth, vague and irrelevant as these seem to you, and (*b*) is not socially unproductive when it does so. I doubt if we can spend our time better on this ride than by giving illustrations of this idea and explaining what it means.

Very well, said Simmias. I wish you'd start by explaining what you mean by an absolute.

The best illustration of an absolutistic quality in our experience, said Cebes, is found when we examine our mental life and see what it implies. The principle of contradiction— the idea that a thing cannot be and not be at the same time —is an example. By the same token consistency of thought is an absolute for every rational person. As I have said before, you cannot deny it for you presuppose it even in your denial. Now you may call this simply a trick of the mind if you wish, but it is such an important trick with such weighty consequences for all of us that you certainly can't laugh it off. Of course you will point out that at most consistency is but a formal principle with no empirical or factual content, but so far would I be from denying this that I would join you in trying to make it clear. The absolute doesn't give us factual details. It offers only general rules for all details. When we try to apply it our difficulties arise out of our imperfect knowledge of facts, but for this I think the absolute itself is not responsible.

Let me try to make this clearer by saying that the difference between absolute and empirical is that one applies to moral attitudes, the other to factual bits of knowledge. Thus, for example, the truth as an ideal is absolute in its claim on us not only (*a*) because we can't argue against it without presupposing it but also (*b*) because we can't think of any *normal* human situation where it is not better to know the truth than to be misled. But our knowledge of any empirical fact is only relative and, at most, probable, because (*a*) it rests on sense experience which is notoriously untrustworthy and (*b*) it represents data about the world of nature which may always be upset when a new scientific experiment is devised. Thus it is an absolute rule that I should always seek the truth, but no empirical truth is ever absolute. We can only be sure that we cannot be sure of empirical knowledge. Yet though we cannot be sure of any empirical fact we can be sure of the moral truth that we should know as many facts as possible. It is therefore in the realm of moral attitudes, or of values, that absolutes come most clearly into view. That knowledge is *better* than ignorance, justice than injustice, and love than hate seems to me to be undeniable. Of course you will object that the real difficulty comes when we try to apply our moral insights, but even here the difficulty is with our imperfect empirical knowledge, not with the insights as such. Is the moral command to love our enemies abrogated simply because we have not sufficient wit or skill or knowledge of the empirical situation to apply it in time of war? I cannot believe that it is. Nor can I believe that the liberal belief in a reason that should always be sought is essentially mistaken.

This is why, as I have tried to show, liberalism seems to me to contribute to our understanding of religion, morals, and education at the same time. We start, as liberals, with a truth about reason. We discover that this implies moral goals. We find that these determine our view of the nature of the divine as the rational good, that is, the reasonable object of our complete devotion, and we go on to try to express the same truth in education by calling that type liberal which sets up the truths of reason as ends in themselves and refuses to be diverted from following them.

I just want to point out that you haven't yet defined reason, said Simmias.

Reason is a coherent interpretation of experience, replied Cebes. As such I agree, of course, that it needs the various empirical details life offers it before it can become complete and full-orbed. But I would stoutly maintain that its standards of consistency have a special quality which is unlike anything we find on the empirical level and which in its distinctiveness passes judgment on the data of empirical life. Of course reason as we experience it most of the time is an active process of discovering facts and weaving them into as harmonious a pattern as possible. But here I am thinking primarily of that aspect of reason which we know as a principle of coherence, a set of logical relationships which judges life and provides rules for it. Many of my neo-orthodox friends claim that reason has something possessive about it and that a reasonable man seeks the good as though it were his private property, whereas the religious man's search for God is free from this taint. For my part, I simply cannot see that this is true. It would appear to me that both types of search may be tainted in the same way. A man may use either reason or religion for base personal ends. But true reason and religion are avenues to what is universal rather than what is private and, as I have said before, the best way to understand this universal quality in religion is to see it in its reasonable aspect.

It still seems to me, said Simmias, that for an educator you have a very narrow view of human nature. The real question for us as teachers is not what reason may be in a far-off ethereal world but what it means to the students trying to put it to work. You talk as though young people came to college ready to search for ideas in all their abstractness and to respond to them when found. Actually they must have a felt need for this sort of training before it can mean anything to them. The person whose abstract ideas are unaccompanied by vivid feelings might as well not have the ideas. Progressive education has taught us that a student will learn well only when he sees how what he learns fits his own purposes and enters into his own notion of what is worth while. Remember also that much of your talk about the detachment of truth fails to recognize the psychological fact that there is no such thing as a detached mental act unaccompanied by a motor response. The real question is how you can shift a student's interest from the level where his response is purely visceral to that where he responds with viscera and cortex both. The classroom should not merely hold up truth as an ideal before the student. It should provide conditions that aid attitudes to ripen and personalities to mature.

You seem to forget, he went on, that a deepening of the emotions themselves is important. Students need security;

they yearn for the feeling that they have a respectable place in society; they must learn to deal creatively with their emotional problems. All this your strictly academic instruction overlooks. Furthermore, the statement: I will be loyal to the truth—period—is without significance. What you mean is: I will be loyal to the truth as I can see it applying to this or that situation—which is something quite different. Actually no one teaches the truth. A good teacher helps the student to become the kind of person who will understand the truth when he sees it—another process entirely. I want to remind you, also, that your much-vaunted reason has a curious way of denying itself. Left to its own resources it always shows what must to you seem like a strange tendency to turn into naturalism, behaviorism, or positivism where what you have been calling the distinctive qualities of mind are left out entirely. Each of these asserts that life is but a mechanical process suffering from the illusion that it is not mechanical.

To me, Simmias concluded, all this points to the hopeless inadequacy of a liberal philosophy or theory of education that tries to bring out the virtues of reason as a special goal or end in itself. Today if ever the empty pretensions of such an effort should lie exposed for everyone to see. Here we are passing through the valley of the shadow of death. Surely you have not been touched by today's despair if you think that men will emerge with a new confidence in reason! For most people life has become a great non-sequitur, a process lived in defiance of reason. If we emerge from the shadow finally it will be with a new and desperate need for sheer animal faith— faith in life, faith in ourselves, faith in our fellow men and in God, faith that the awful agony of human experience can be endured and that something worth while will come out of it all. This is what people will crave, and both religion and education should prepare accordingly.

Just then the car reached the Hillsgrove airport and the two men boarded the plane for New Haven. I have a peculiar sense of release remarked Cebes as they started, whenever I take to the air. The easy sweep upward after jouncing along on the ground brings one of the most unfettering sensations I know anything about. It gives me an unutterable sense of mastery and helps me to rise above the turmoil of life in more ways than one.

What I think about, said Simmias, is the fact that I have to come back to earth, and I always breathe a silent prayer that the return may be in harmony with the empirical conditions on the landing field. This flight will be successful only so long as we are aware of what is happening there. So I do beg you to guard your views of education from too detached an excursion into the unknown. Does liberal education really keep in touch with what we know are the salient facts of life? Isn't verbalism always tricky? Don't we tend to produce in students' minds sterile formulas when what we need is brave decisions based on living emotions?

There is such a thing as perspective, replied Cebes, looking down at the landscape, and it has its own uses even though they are not always obvious. You may remember the ship's captain who was awakened by a terrific crash and rushed to the bridge, crying to the sailor at the helm, "Didn't I tell you to set your course by the North Star?" "Oh, yes," replied the sailor, "but we passed that long ago." Now the truth as an ideal to steer by, or reason as a set of rules to observe, is like the North Star. It points a general direction for our thought; it maintains its relation to us as we go forward and corrects us when we are out of line. As a guide for our reflection it is like the principle of experimentalism in science, keeping us open-minded and free from alliances that would entangle us too quickly. That is why it seems to me that there should always be a place for liberal teaching which refuses to define its aims in any other terms. But to keep our course plotted by the North Star doesn't mean that we should neglect the shoals and reefs or that this plane, for example, should be oblivious to conditions on the ground, any more than the advice to lift up our eyes unto the hills means that we should neglect the valleys of decision. The liberal has never meant that nor does liberal education mean it now. Let me try to explain this by pointing first to the impossibility of defining educational goals except in terms of the truth and then showing what I think the principle of alternation means when applied to education.

To begin with, you have spoken of the curious way reason has of defeating itself by turning into naturalism, behaviorism, and the like. I would reply that it is not reason that does this but an arbitrary limitation of reason to the scientific handling of sense data. When at the start you rule out any knowledge but that based on sense experiences and any kind of data but that which the world of empirical nature provides, of course you won't get far in your attempts to reach the world of moral values. As you well know, I believe that we have experiences which show us the significance of insight into the nature of love and of truth and that these experiences of value when properly safeguarded are as able to give us knowledge as is the scientific manipulation of sense data. When you interpret reason in this broader way it doesn't defeat itself. In fact it is the effort to limit reason to the narrower field that turns self-defeating. I have seen this occur in education over and over again.

For example, what happens to these various attempts to define liberal education in terms of special purposes? It wasn't so long ago that people wanted colleges to define their goal as that of making students more religious. Well, I want them to be religious as much as the next man does but, as I said before, I think you have to approach these matters with subtlety. I'm not sure that you make students more religious by constantly parading the aims of religion before them and intimating that the only aspect of truth with which you are concerned is that which bears on the religious life. Like character, religion is caught and not taught. Sometimes we best serve its ends by not preaching them too continuously. The college's primary concern, as I see it, is to teach its students to reverence the truth. If it does this in the right way it can trust the students themselves to recognize the relation of truth to God and the claim a God of truth has on us.

A similar problem appears when people talk about education for character or good citizenship. Will any person in his right mind deny that we want our students to have character and to be good citizens? But how do you educate for these ends in college? Do the well-meaning people who want the colleges to define their goals this way themselves know what character and good citizenship are? Don't they often mean that they want students to share *their* ideas of character and good citizenship by refraining from their pet vices like dancing or card playing and voting as they do the straight Republican ticket? Yet, isn't it really the job of the college to prepare for citizenship in a *changing* world and doesn't this mean stretching our students' minds to meet new conditions and to form moral judgments on new facts? These people with their special ends for education often make me think of the kindly classicists who argue for Latin and Greek because they were themselves brought up on them. I believe it was Stephen Leacock who said, "When they talk of what Vergil did for them, one sometimes wishes he hadn't done it!" After all, how can we better prepare for good citizenship through a liberal arts education than by arousing a passion for reason which means also for justice?

But even Hitler had a passion for what he thought was justice, interrupted Simmias. That helps to explain why I am so terribly suspicious of these absolutists. They are fanatics and troublemakers who haven't been curbed by the facts and they become so dangerous because they are allowed just the kind of leeway with abstract ideas that you apparently would give them. I'm all for good sound empirical and workable compromises based on knowledge of what the immediate situation demands and I think any education that neglects this is headed for trouble.

Again let me point out, said Cebes, that you are rushing to unsound conclusions about liberalism because you fail to see that the word "liberal" applies to one element in a total context. Just as freedom even in human life arises in a context of experiences, many of which are completely determined, so the goal of liberal education as the search for truth arises in a total situation which also presents many other educational aims. Notice, for example, that the college is only one among many teaching agencies. The home, the school, the church, have their own jobs to do. The college has its particular goal only because it can presuppose their work. Not only have you no right but you certainly have not the ability to seek the truth as a special end unless you have the character and sense of responsibility that these others should have developed. Also, as I shall try to show later, you should not engage in this special activity unless you make particular provision for other activities that will promote social decisiveness and responsibility.

Even the particular virtues stressed by the liberal college, such as intellectual honesty, mean what they do and occupy their special place in life only because they presuppose other virtues that are as important. Look at the different meanings the word honesty itself accumulates for the normal boy in the course of his growth. When he is quite young it means not telling lies and not cheating. A little later it takes on a more positive coloring and refers to paying one's bills promptly and speaking out truthfully on moot questions instead of merely refraining from falsehood. To the college student the phrase "intellectual honesty" opens up wider vistas. He begins to see that it requires much more than the merely negative avoidance of contradiction. Soon he is fired by enthusiasm for Truth with a capital T and for all the new ranges of experience to which it beckons. Intellectual honesty becomes a spiritual passion disclosing to him the world of things that should be in all its glaring contrast to things as they are. The search for truth thus gives him both an exciting feeling of discovery and a triumphant sense of mission. This in turn leads him, or should lead him at its best, to want to apply truth to human affairs. And that, as I see it, is where the training in facts becomes especially important because that is where a knowledge of facts makes a special contribution to his intellectual development. Of course I don't mean that he isn't constantly learning facts all along the way. I mean simply that these social facts that you emphasize so much will really become significant for the student when the passion for truth as such has once been aroused.

This, you see, is the principle of alternation applied to education. There is a time for arousing enthusiasm for the truth in all the detachment we can achieve for it and there is also a time for putting it to work in the battle for social righteousness. The balance between them is very delicate and we have no adequate formula for it. But I should like to point to two instances of the way it works in college which may help us to understand the general principle itself. One of these has to do with the teaching of religion, the other with the social purposes of ideas.

I've said, for example, that in college we should teach religion by teaching the truth, and I believe we can. Yet obviously this is an incomplete statement. "Ye shall know the truth and the truth shall make you free." But as Aldous Huxley says, ye shall know the truth and it shall also make you mad. In other words, not all truth-teaching is religious, nor is all religious teaching a sheer intellectual quest for the truth. Your own claim that emotions must be trained is certainly in point, and much truth that is taught has no obvious bearing on religion. Further, it is particularly clear on the college level that when the student is initiated into the mysteries and the glories of freedom of inquiry we must not let him feel that the dice are loaded and that we allow him only the kind of inquiry that will result in religious belief.

We find ourselves, then, in this dilemma. We have faith in the truth and we are eager to expose our students to it. But, as you have pointed out, we see so many examples of human frailty, and especially of human propensity to use books and learning as an escape from responsible living, that to guard the truth itself we have to take measures to strengthen the human beings who are exposed to its influence. As careful educators we should do all we can to encourage their moral purposefulness and to make up for the one-sided verbalism of the kind of truth we expose them to in college. Further, we are agreed that real freedom is freedom to choose the good and that this presupposes some experience of the good. Consequently in all our college work we should distinguish two educational agencies—the curriculum on the one hand and the community on the other. The free search for ideas in the classroom should be supplemented by agencies in the community which offer a chance for the application of ideas. Thus, for example, the tentativeness and balanced judgment required in the curriculum should be rounded out by the decisions made in the religious activities carried on by the community.

In some such way as this I believe a liberal college should try to correct the one-sidedness into which it may so easily lapse and I would contend that when it does so it is not false but rather in the highest degree faithful to its own liberal ideal. Now let me turn to the illustration from the teaching of social truths. Here again both the college and the larger industrial community outside the college walls can be made to furnish chances for responsible social action. But I'm thinking now especially of discussions in the classroom and of the fact that very frequently the instructor will be able to show how the academic interest and the social interest supplement each other. A student will not learn less algebra and geometry, for instance, if a skillful teacher points out that mathematics exemplifies the universality of the laws of mind and their applicability to all rational beings of whatever race or creed. He will not be deterred from exploring the more abstract possibilities of science if he is shown that science itself with its constant appeal to social verification is the great coöperative achievement of our time. Nor will he be made blind to the more esoteric values in the study of literature if he sees how complete among thoughtful men of all ages is the agreement as to the worth of the great masterpieces. Further, since the teaching of history is in any case a selective process, no violence will be done to the facts by focusing attention on history as the record of men's struggles throughout the years to build a just and democratic social order.

In other words, if one grants, as I think we both do, that education has many aims and that the service of society ranks high among them, it is still a fact that the colleges should define their goal in terms of free inquiry. It is also a fact that this goal is less one-sided than we sometimes suppose and in particular that it is less limiting than your goal of social usefulness. There is something about usefulness as an end which always proves unsatisfactory. This is the trouble that all pragmatisms and utilitarianisms run into, no matter how fair is their appearance at the start. Sooner or later they find it hard to answer questions about usefulness for what or usefulness by whose standards and too often they end by eliminating truth as a special goal altogether. On the other hand truth, though it may at first blush seem more limited, actually is a broader and more productive educational aim, particularly when care is taken to supplement it in the way I have indicated. Put in its most elemental terms, the difference appears, I think, when you observe the change that comes over many a boy who is exposed to the influence of liberal education at its best. He comes to college with the vague idea that he wants to learn the truth so that he can use it for his own purposes. He leaves with a vision of the purposes the truth has for him. When that happens the liberal ideal has demonstrated what it is and what it can do.

I have already shown that I have no real quarrel with your desire to put education to work for society. I simply think my way of doing it is better. Now I want to come over further to your side by admitting that many of your criticisms of liberalism as a selfish philosophy have been true in the past. No one can deny that for a long time it was tainted with individualism of an excessive type. But today the old laissez faire and competitive liberalism is dead and surely no thoughtful person wants to revive it. Like democracy itself liberalism has found the social meaning implicit in its own genius. For example, where democracy used to talk of the rights of the individual we now consider it proper that it should focus its attention on the free society. Instead of defining freedom of speech today as the right any man has to talk on any subject anywhere, we say that society has the right to hear all sides of all important questions. Liberalism has taken a similar turn.

So I think you should see that in all my talk of "reason" as a goal for liberal education I am assuming that the pressures of our time have forced us to realize the social implications of reason and that it is no longer possible for an honest man to use the search for truth as an escape into irresponsibility. The very methods that liberal education employs have lost their individualistic emphasis. Even the standard illustration of Mark Hopkins on a log has become outmoded. Today we think of education as an experience of learning in a group. Each college depends on its community life to provide excitement, stimulus, and a contagious enthusiasm for ideas. You and I may yet live to see a student body swept off its feet as readily by a brilliant solution for an intellectual problem as by a football victory. When that day dawns the college community as an educational force will have come into its own. And while we are indulging in prophecy I should like to affirm also that fifty years from now the college that builds walls between itself and the industrial community at its doors and allows the walls to become covered with Japanese ivy will be neglected by society as a relic of bygone times. All this, you see, is in line with my main thesis that reason is one element in a larger context of experience and that the education of the intellect must be supplemented by training of other sorts. It was Professor Whitehead, you recall, who said that "Great readers, who exclude other activities, are not distinguished by subtlety of brain. They tend to be timid, conventional thinkers." And wasn't it Thomas Hobbes who remarked that if he had read as many books as other men he would be as ignorant as they?

One might use those quotations as a plea for more vocational education, observed Simmias, especially when you couple with them Professor Whitehead's other remark that "the disuse of hand-craft is a contributory cause to the brain lethargy of aristocracies."

Of course it points to more vocational education, said Cebes, but I think you will agree that what Professor Whitehead wants is to have the barriers between liberal and vocational education broken down. As he has often affirmed, education should turn out the pupil with something he knows well and something he can do well. The two processes are interwoven. Even on a purely utilitarian level it is a question whether a man should be trained for one vocation when nobody can tell enough about the future to know whether that vocation will be needed. You yourself have shifted from teaching to government work, and millions of other men have changed their occupations because of the war. As Socrates used to say, we want to teach not merely the special skills men learn as shipbuilders and flute-players but the basic knowledge that all men need in general.

So far colleges have taught what no man needs in particular, said Simmias.

The trouble, replied Cebes, is that we have not fully understood the general needs of men and further we have not understood how artificial is the barrier between liberal and vocational if we erect it in terms of subject matter. It is often pointed out that Hebrew and Greek were vocational subjects when colleges were training schools for the ministry. Now they seem so remote from actual life that we classify them as liberal because that is what we think liberal implies. French and German, conversely, were considered liberal subjects until the war when they became desperately vocational. Doesn't this show that the word "liberal" itself needs to be clarified? Perhaps it should be applied not to subject matter but to methods of teaching. What of the sciences, for example; are they liberal or vocational? Isn't it a question of the way they are taught? I cannot think that a topic becomes illiberal just because it is studied in preparation for a profession. Certainly there is nothing undignified, and I hope nothing illiberal, in preparing a man for his life's work. That is why I should say a subject is taught liberally when the student is led through it to an understanding of some of the deeper concerns of human life. We shouldn't think of the sciences as remote from humane and liberal values, or, on the other hand, of the more humanistic disciplines as having no bearing on practical life.

You're coming dangerously close to my position, said Simmias.

I've always had the feeling that we might draw nearer together if we could make our ideas clearer, said Cebes. Let me proceed in this irenic vein a little further. As you remarked earlier, a great deal of harm has been done by drawing a sharp line between the gentleman who works, if at all, with his eyes over a book and the laborer who uses his hands. But today this contrast means less than it did. Modern labor is becoming more technical. There is little doubt that more and more the backbreaking tasks will be taken over by machines. The laboratory should, and in all probability will, reach out farther into the fields, the mines, and the various industries to ease the load placed on men's muscles. What I seem to see is an ever greater attempt to infuse the liberal and humane spirit into the work of mechanic, artisan, and technician. Each of these should become aware of the human values to which his work contributes, and each can be made so by the right kind of education. In our colleges, therefore, we shall be less and less concerned whether we are teaching pure or applied science. It will all be applied sooner or later. But we shall want to teach science liberally, with an eye for what it implies, as well as for how it is applied, hoping our students will see more deeply into what nature is as well as what they themselves must do.

Thus our future education will accomplish two results. It will make our industrial workers aware of the larger significance of the forces they deal with, while the white-collar men will understand better what keeps their collars white and what makes the wheels go round, or especially what makes them stop when you are far from a garage. All that I as a liberal am contending for is the need for keeping our educational sights lifted. You may remember that in the Sanskrit language the word *nama* or "name" is sometimes used to express the magical power one gains by the use of a word or formula. At such times the name is used for the selfish interests of the one who knows it. At other times it means what Socrates meant by *eidos*, namely, that in a thing which makes it what it is. In this sense to know its name is to give it power over us or to make us aware of the claim it exercises. An example is when we see that we value justice not because it is pleasant or useful but simply and solely because it is justice. I think education should make clear to us this aspect of words and their meaning.

I wish you would be more specific than you have been so far, said Simmias, and tell just what it is that the college should teach.

If I can define its general aims, said Cebes, I think the details will look out for themselves. Furthermore, it is wholly proper that they should change with the rapid march of events. But surely no one can be out of sympathy today with the many attempts to give the curriculum a more organic character and to eliminate the patchwork of credits that so often has passed for education. The tendency toward more requirements and fewer electives is also sound. The college should express its own convictions as to what is worth studying and the students should work at a common core of subject matter if for no other reason than to gain the feeling of being engaged in a common intellectual enterprise.

With regard to the subjects that can provide this unity—of course my prejudices would call first for philosophy as an inquiry into the general ideas with which man as a rational being is concerned, and also for history as a record of the organic growth of culture. Philosophy doesn't answer all our questions, but part of its virtue lies in the problems it raises and the discontent it breeds with easy answers. Of course philosophy alone is not enough. Along with its abstractions the student should be given plenty of facts as one way of bridging the chasm between thought and action. But if abstractions without facts are empty, certainly facts without the possibilities inherent in abstractions are blind.

As for history—the term covers so much that it is hard to satisfy your passion for concreteness in discussing it. But I should like to have a college curriculum organized around history in such a way that the student sees all his subjects as stemming from one historical matrix. On one side, to speak figuratively, come the sciences, as man's attempts to understand and control nature. On the other are the languages, literatures, and arts, as part of his attempt to express, communicate, and record his ideas and deepest emotions. In the middle are the political and economic institutions he has worked out for his social life and at the very center the philosophies and religions which represent his most intimate thought about himself and his relation to his world.

So far as the sciences are concerned, I would simply say first that I wish our colleges would provide more courses for the liberal arts student who will not make science his profession; and second, I wish that the student could be encouraged to distinguish between science as a body of knowledge and science as a method of inquiry. The forces of destruction it now provides point up the fact that we no longer can treat scientific research as of neutral import and as having no relation to man's cherished values. We must recall and emphasize anew the truth that scientific inquiry is itself a moral enterprise demanding not only intelligence but such moral qualities as discipline, asceticism, disinterestedness, courage, and above all, coöperativeness. Science ought to furnish one of our best devices for moral instruction. We must use it to this end before it is too late.

About the languages, I would remark merely that we should begin them earlier if we study them at all. Real familiarity with one language is worth far more than a nodding acquaintance with two. So many personal qualities depend on our powers of expression that knowledge of a new language develops the personality itself in a manner that is unique. The other devices now in use which further student expression are of course admirable. Individualized instruction, greater student participation in the classroom, and methods to enable the gifted student to get ahead rapidly are wholly in order. I like these various attempts to coördinate vacation activities and college work. All the teaching techniques provided by films and records and models, to say nothing of field trips and excursions, should prove revolutionary. But I must register my protest against the expression "student-centered education." To give the student the idea that education centers in him instead of in the truth seems to me to adopt the best possible means of blocking his insight from the start. A liberally educated man is one who has seen what truth demands and adjusted his life to it.

There was silence for a few moments, broken only by the steady hum of the motors.

Finally Simmias remarked abruptly: Milton, thou shouldst be living at this hour! The world hath need of thee! I happened to think of Milton, he said half apologetically, because of the anniversary of the *Areopagitica* and also because Milton is such a good example of a liberal who could make up his mind. He had ideas and a program. He believed in Plato's world of values and in the rule of reason. But he was also active in politics. I wonder how many Miltons are mute and inglorious today because their education has not shown them how to translate their ideas into action.

Milton should indeed be living, replied Cebes. I could not help thinking of another whom we need as much. Have you noticed how near Socrates has been at times and yet how far away he has remained? He has been near in the sense that you and I, along with all who have read about him, could not help catching some of his spirit. Yet he has stayed far away in that we have lacked his ability to analyze our problems and to see what should be done about them. Socrates hardly needed these moral supplements to liberal education that you have stressed and that I have agreed are necessary. For him to see the truth was to act on it because his nature was organized that way. But with all our limitations even you and I can feel how necessary it is for the world to try to rise to his level and to see ideas as he saw them. How eagerly does mankind search today for a set of conceptions that will make clear the real agreement in its aims, the unity of its life, the bound-togetherness of its condition! How desperately we cry out for the revelation of our common lot as one family of nations who are driven apart by our lusts and our pride but who yet can be knit together in the presence of an idea that all can see and share!

Do you remember our talk, in the other two conversations, of the need for passing from the level of mechanical to that of reasonable necessity? he went on. Another character from ancient times made that transition in such a way as to bring out its significance for our common life as men. In the eighth century B.C. Amos of Tekoa, working at his sycamore trees, watched the coming of summer fruit. He speculated on the power that made the seven stars and Orion, that turned the shadow of death into morning and made the day dark with night, that raised the waters of the sea and poured them forth on the earth, and he said to himself: This constant force at work in nature must be God. Then he became one of the world's first liberals. It must be at work in history also, he said, but there it must operate as justice and reason, in complete indifference to the capriciousness of men's desires, but in complete accord with rational thought. So Amos heard God say: Are you not as the children of the Ethiopians unto me? It is true that I brought you out of Egypt, but have I not also brought the Philistines from Caphtor and the Syrians from Kir? Because reason is free from favoritism and has the inexorableness of gravitation itself, justice will roll down as waters and righteousness as a mighty stream.

Amos used this insight, you will recall, to explain not only the privileges shared by all nations alike but the rights of the ordinary man. In your special feast days and assemblies, he said to the priests of Bethel, you have made religion into a force that divides men from each other. Behind a screen of particularistic religious observances you have tried to hide your exploitation of the poor. But I come to you as a herdsman, with no education for my vocation as prophet, and no special training in cult or ritual, to preach the liberal truth that the worship of the God of justice should emphasize the universal human values which all men share as men.

It is true that Amos proclaimed a religion for all right-minded men, said Simmias, and that he stood unequivocally for social justice. It is possible also that he had some of our colleges in mind when he said, "The houses of ivory shall perish." I want to point out, however, that the universal imbedded in human experience is not merely rational but may be found on the deeper level of the emotions. Amos' great contemporary Hosea stressed it without resorting to any of the intellectualism that has antagonized people to liberals all through the ages. You will recall that Hosea drew a parable from his own experience of suffering and used it as a symbol of the unity men may win through pain and love. I speak to you, he said in effect, not as priest or prophet or prince (though he could have claimed to be all three), nor even as Jew, but as a man to men, on the basis of my experience as husband and father, and in the light of the family relationship that all men share. I would say to you, Hosea went on, that man who is born to love is born to suffer also, but that in his awareness of suffering as the common lot of man, he may discover the nature of God. I sometimes wonder, Simmias added, whether this is not the deepest lesson our age can learn. Here is an entire world lacerated by suffering greater in extent than it has ever known before. It may be that their raw nerves and harassed feelings will drive men apart into warring groups, so that the conflict will last on in one form or another for years to come. But it is also possible that in their common agony men will be drawn to one another and find themselves developing together the kind of political and economic habits that lead to peace. Should not education strive for this above all? he asked.

Would you say, perhaps, asked Cebes without answering him, that Amos is like the scientist in generalizing from particular events in nature, whereas Hosea like the artist is able to reveal the universal quality in the single emotional experience?

Yes, said Simmias, and although Amos' range is broader, I think Hosea's insight goes deeper. Using your own account of the difference between the probabilities of science and the absoluteness of certain emotional attitudes I would say that on the whole I prefer the emotion of the artist. He may not be so articulate and, as you said before, he may not be able to step outside the mood of the moment to the metaphysical statement, but in that mood he finds more of significance than I, at least, have ever been able to learn from metaphysics. That is why I felt you were a little hard on Tschaikowsky in our last conversation. These profoundly romantic sentiments are not easily translated into words, but the feelings which bind human beings together go back much further in history than the spoken word and link us with our subhuman ancestors and even with the impersonal forces of the cosmos itself. The energies of creation are still at work in our instincts and emotions. In our blood we carry the memories of that day when the morning stars sang together and all the sons of God shouted for joy.

The trouble with liberals, he continued, after a pause, is that they talk too much. A few years ago it would not have been unfair to say that "Man the Thinker," chin on hand with wrinkled brow, occupied an honorable if somewhat aloof position above the common walks of life. Today, however, he has stepped down from his pedestal. People in general are inclined to identify him with "Man the Talker," and talk, through its association with propaganda and such obviously unreliable advertising as we hear over the radio, is now considered of doubtful value. Even among philosophers it is widely believed that speech has been led astray by its own subtlety and has betrayed the cause of truth. With the rise first of pragmatism and then of logical positivism the emphasis has shifted to "Man the Doer" in the sense either of worker for results or manipulator of experimental apparatus and physical stuff. This is why theology, in a similar revolt against abstract thought, calls for a more vigorous figure and tries to fix our attention on "Man the Sinner." But I think that perhaps "Man the Sufferer" is the most appropriate symbol for our time, just as it is central for Christianity. Charles Péguy brought out the binding quality in suffering when he wrote:

> The Son has taken upon himself all the sins of the world
> And the mother all the grief.

But suffering is the great unifier, Simmias went on, because it leads both to insight and to love. Kierkegaard testifies: "One must have suffered very much in the world and have been very uncomfortable before there can even be any talk of loving one's neighbor." After the death of his infant son William James wrote in a letter: "It brings one closer to all mankind—this world old experience." Unamuno adds: "Suffering is that which unites all living beings together; it is the universal or divine blood that flows through us all."

I would be the last to deny what you say, replied Cebes. Yet I might point out that whereas suffering may lead to love it may also lead to bitterness and to distortion. That is why it would seem to me that even more important than "Man the Sufferer" is "Man the Seer" and that here we have a figure in the presence of which we can join hands. Of course the liberal has too often been merely a talker and of course we are suspicious of the glibness of talk in this age which combines untold heights of heroism and untold depths of agony. But the liberal's words and his talk have been his way of correcting his prejudices by the appeal to reason, and the attempt was worth while even though it was not always crowned with success. You will recall how Socrates used to set us conversing and how well Plato recorded the spirit of our talk. Yet for both Socrates and

Plato the highest human experience was not talk but *theoria;* that is, insight, vision, understanding. And surely you and I would agree that this is the great aim of education today. We started out to ask whether ideas had any place in a world so obviously controlled by violence. We went on to say that mind is buffeted about by social forces, is circumscribed by uncounted bodily factors, is thwarted by the obduracy of physical nature and the just plain orneriness of selfish men. But truth still has its influence when the conditions are right, and the method of persuasion still has its power when men are prepared for it. In the beginning was the word, not the deed as some have tried to say, and the word became flesh, not stone. It is a growing word and in the right environment it flourishes. Part of our job, we would agree, is to prepare the ground and to make sure that the seed falls upon good soil.

All this adds up to two important truths that I hope liberal education will take to heart. First, our colleges must recover the sense of mission they had when many of them were founded. At that time the purpose was to save souls from perdition; now it is to save society from the results of its own unreasonableness. I cannot believe that this latter is any less important or any less powerful as an incentive than the former.

In the second place we must take specific account of the extraordinary reinforcement that has come to the aid of our moral teaching. I refer to nothing else than the atomic bomb. Today as never before we face in its dazzling clarity a fact which we should have known all along—I mean the utter incompatibility of civilization and war. At last selfish and social purposes have merged. When we work to free society from the curse of unbridled competition we are working at the same time for our survival as individuals. Coöperation has finally come into its own as both a reasonable ideal and a practical need.

Above all, let's listen no longer to those strident voices insisting that human nature will not change, that wars are inevitable, and that there is nothing new under the sun. You and I both realize that during the individual life span and in the right kind of environment human nature changes constantly. This must furnish the basic tenet for our creed as educators. We have seen it change under the impact of war, of suffering, of frustration. We have also seen it change under the influence of hope, of love, and of ideas. When these forces of reason are mixed with a healthy fear of the annihilation that will follow failure, the combination should bring results undreamed of in any educational philosophy so far known.

Both men were silent for several moments. Finally Simmias looked out of the window. There's East Rock, he exclaimed. There's Yale, he said, a minute later. The plane flew on and, as if to give them a special thrill, circled over the Yale campus.

Do you notice the two styles of architecture? asked Simmias. See the Gothic with all its signs of tension. The massive bulk combined with the fragile pillars and the ascending lines gives the feeling, as Ralph Adams Cram once said, of flinging its passion against the sky. Gothic is the architecture of both motion and emotion—that is what makes it so powerfully appealing.

I prefer the light and freedom of the Colonial, said Cebes, perhaps because it reminds me of the Athens of the older days. I notice also, he added, that when it built the Divinity School Yale chose Colonial architecture, even though the Gothic traditionally has been so close to religion.

Certainly the two are different, said Simmias. Does this

mean that you and I must remain apart without real understanding of each other?

You know we shouldn't allow that suggestion to take root in
our minds, said Cebes. Gothic and Colonial speak to varying
moods but the area in which they share is greater than that in
which they differ. Each can provide an appropriate environment for what we believe in. Both are beautiful, both speak of
the noble past, each in its own way lifts us above the common-
place and the sordid. The reason they are opposed so sharply
as we look down on them is that they are set over against each
other in space, and space, as you well know, has never done
justice to quality. You will recall that Cornford shows how the
Olympian religion on which we were brought up was spatially
oriented in that its gods ruled over well-marked provinces. This
is one real reason why it turned into the materialism of Democ-
ritus, where the units of reality were spatial atoms. But you and
I live in time as well as in space. We provide living evidence
of the truth of the old Orphic theories that quality develops in
the religion that is oriented to time, the kind of religion that
takes account of the growth of the soul in the round of the
seasons and the round of rebirths. As Christianity would put it,
the importance of the Cross lies in the fact that it is not the end
but that it points beyond itself, and we feel the force of the
insight even though we do not know how to define just what
that beyond includes.

So it is that you and I living in time and in the midst of
memories which we partially remake every day can grow
toward each other and share a common life, as objects that are
merely in space cannot. Plato felt the binding force of this time
element, I think. That was why he reported our conversations
in such lengthy detail. A conversation is a good symbol of the

kind of unity in diversity that life seems to offer. At the beginning of our talk back there in the North Station you said that life is a series of partings and that we meet but to part again. But when we meet in a common purpose we don't part. This unity stays with us because it brings a larger idea in which we both participate and which makes it possible for us to share in the lives of men of good will of every age.

One final word, he added. Today's tragedy should help us both to understand the kind of control that idea exercises over life. Certainly we can no longer think of human beings as responding only to the pleasurable stimulus of the moment. When you see how these boys met the challenge of war you can't believe that life is lived only for enjoyment, and when you think of the fact that their danger and death meant our safety and peace you have a new and very disturbing sense of what the word responsibility means. What seems therefore to be coming vaguely to consciousness in the minds of a great many people is the idea that life is lived for the sake of what is above life, and that suffering must be endured on behalf of a greater good and a larger truth than we have yet been able to grasp. Should not the education of the future bind all men together in the search for this truth? he asked.

Let us work as well as pray for this end, said Simmias as they drew nearer the field.

———————————

The plane was just about to make a perfect three-point landing when Simmias found himself looking up at the pillars of the Parthenon with Cebes, waking from a sound sleep, beside him. What an extraordinary dream! he said. I thought I was projected into the 392nd Olympiad. They called it A.D. 1945, and you were there too.

So I was, said Cebes.

How amazing that we should have shared the same dream! Simmias went on. Yet, after all, it is dreams that men share. The separation comes when they return to the grim facts of reality. Or need it? he asked. If our dream was right, may not growth through time and increasing maturity draw men nearer together? But tell me, he said, do you suppose the world will ever be as bad as it seemed in that dream?

No matter how bad it becomes, said Cebes, it is not completely unredeemed while men have a passion for the truth and for the unity that the truth can bring.

And I have enough faith in human nature, added Simmias, to believe that it will always provide at least a few men who have the courage to do what the truth requires. With this he stood up, stretched himself, and, after a brief farewell, made his way down from the Acropolis, past the Areopagus to his home in the city on the plain.

Cebes remained on the hill looking off at the amethystine haze over Hymettus as it showed through the Parthenon columns. Finally he bowed his head. Lead us out of the cave, he murmured, O God of Truth. Help us to realize our common task as men, in whatever land or age our lot is cast. Make our words flower in deeds and help us through both to realize the unity that is ours since we are thine. And grant to each of us the understanding heart which, as thou didst reveal to the wise man of old, is the surest pledge that all things else will be added.